CHRISTMAS (handwritten)

KENTUCKY

One Tank Trips

WITH DENNY TREASE

JACKIE, ROBIN, BO (handwritten)

FIRST EDITION

Facts, maps, directions & other details
on 55 intriguing Kentucky destinations

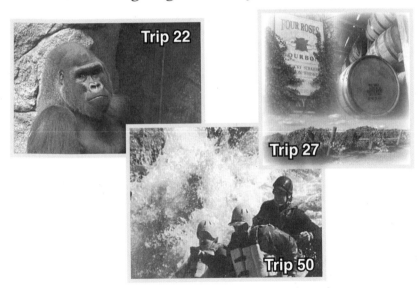

Trip 22

Trip 27

Trip 50

Publishers

Back Home In Kentucky, Inc.
Jerlene Rose & William E. Matthews
and
The Clark Group
Robert G. Clark & Florence S. Huffman

Cover Design & Photo Editor
Sid Webb, Sid Webb Photography

Editors
Florence S. Huffman, Jerlene Rose

Design & Composition
Kelly Elliott

Sales & Marketing
William E. Matthews, Robert G. Clark, Sam Stephens & Stan Taulbee

Production
Jennifer Kash, Renee Miller & Carla Bryan

Order additional copies by calling: (800) 944-3995 or (606) 663-1011
Order online: http://store.kyalmanac.com

Back Home In Kentucky, Inc.
P.O. Box 710, Clay City, KY 40312
(606) 663-1011
www.backhomeinky.com • info@backhomeinky.com

The Clark Group
P.O. Box 24766, Lexington, KY 40524
(800) 944-3995 (859) 233-7623
www.kyalmanac.com • info@theclarkgroupinfo.com

ISBN: 1-883589-76-2

While we have made every effort to ensure the accuracy of all information included in this publication, the publishers cannot accept responsibility for errors or omissions which may occur. All admission prices and opening times are based on information given to us at press time. All prices quoted are without tax. Please be sure to call ahead before your trip because **admission fees and hours may change.**
We welcome your comments and suggestions for future editions of this publication.

Quantity purchases of Kentucky One Tank Trips are available to book stores, gift shops, distributors and wholesalers.

Special thanks to: WKYT-TV Channel 27; Sid Webb; Marcheta Sparrow, Kentucky Tourism Council; AAA; Kentucky Horse Park; Kentucky Transportation Cabinet; Kentucky Dept. of Parks; Kentucky Dept. of Tourism and our advertisers.

Kentucky One Tank Trips tells the stories of fun destinations, attractions and events across Kentucky — that you can reach on one tank of gas. This publication is a joint-venture of **Back Home In Kentucky, Inc.** and **The Clark Group**. We designed One Tank Trips to enhance your travel experience. With over 52 destinations you can take one trip for every weekend of the year.

In recent years the rising price of gas has been a continual topic of conversation...rather like the weather in Kentucky. One Tank Trips presents readers with trips to make their leisure travel easy, entertaining and less expensive. People like to sightsee, hike and camp, visit historic places, eat good food, shop, and sometimes, just lie around doing nothing. This guide has something for everyone.

Whether you are new to the Bluegrass State, or have lived here all your life, Kentucky One Tank Trips is a perfect guide to true Kentucky treasures. Each book is packed with information: how to get there, admission prices, hours of operation and web site addresses. This handy guide belongs in every glove compartment.

WKYT-TV Channel 27 will air segments about Kentucky One Tank Trips. With host Denny Trease's enthusiasm for Kentucky and sharp eye for fun trips, his show is bound to entertain.

Enjoy the book and be sure to watch WKYT-TV Channel 27 where One Tank Trips are featured. By the way, we'd love to hear from you about your trips; log on to one of our web sites and share your experiences with us.

Back Home In Kentucky Inc.
William E. Matthews

The Clark Group
Robert G. Clark

Table of Contents

Table of Contents

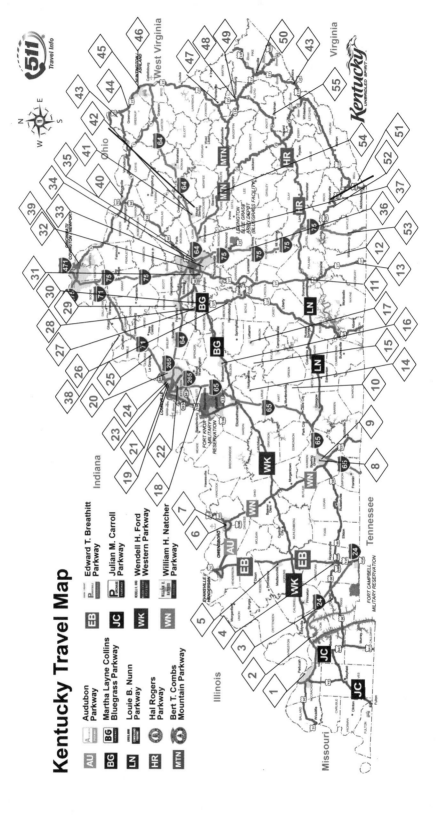

Kentucky Travel Map

AU — Audubon Parkway
BG — Martha Layne Collins Bluegrass Parkway
LN — Louie B. Nunn Parkway
HR — Hal Rogers Parkway
MTN — Bert T. Combs Mountain Parkway

EB — Edward T. Breathitt Parkway
JC — Julian M. Carroll Parkway
WK — Wendell H. Ford Western Parkway
WN — William H. Natcher Parkway

Trip Numbers Map Index

Alphabetical Index

Denny Trease

WKYT-TV Channel 27 News is excited to sponsor the first edition of Kentucky **One Tank Trips**. Emmy-winning reporter Denny Trease is your host for a series of news segments featuring **One Tank Trips** to Kentucky attractions, events and leisure travel destinations. This guide is very timely as friends and families plan trips. Kentuckians, like many Americans, are taking shorter vacations and the new **One Tank Trips** book is going to be a huge hit as everyone struggles with ever-rising gas prices.

You will enjoy Denny Trease as your "travel host." Denny is in his second stint at Lexington's WKYT-TV, the most watched television station in Central Kentucky. Denny, a veteran of more than 30 years in broadcasting, spent eight seasons as the play-by-play television voice of the Kentucky Wildcats in basketball and football beginning in 1972. Denny then moved to Kansas City to call major league baseball games on the KC Royal's eight-state television network. On returning to his beloved Bluegrass State in 2000, Denny moved into news reporting and launched a popular feature called "Trease's Travels." **One Tank Trips** is a natural extension of his travels across Kentucky.

We are expecting an enthusiastic response to our **One Tank Trips** news segments. Log on to www.wkyttv.com to view our on-air stories. Enjoy the book, have fun and be sure to watch WKYT-TV Channel 27 News for even more **One Tank Trips**.

Take advantage of what more than **48 million** members already know:

AAA membership is more than just Roadside Assistance.

Join AAA Today

avel Agency Services - Insurance Produc
- Driving Directions - Discount Attraction
Tickets - Fuel Price Finder - aaa.com -
oriegn Currency - Maps and Tourbooks
Hertz - Show Your Card & Save - Travel
ore - Cruises- Emergency Road Service
el Agency Services - Insurance Prod
riving Directions - Discount Attracti
kets - Fuel Price Finder - aaa.co
Currency - Maps and Tourb
Show Your Card & Save
e - Cruises- Emerge
Road Servic

From free TripTik® Routings that get you where you're going and TourBook® guides help you decide where to stay and what to do along the way to Insurance Products, Travel Agency Services, and Financial Service Products, *AAA membership is so much more than what you may think!* Join Today!

VISIT
Kentucky National Historical Parks & Historic Sites

ABRAHAM LINCOLN
BIRTHPLACE NATIONAL
HISTORIC SITE
http://www.nps.gov/abli/

BIG SOUTH FORK NATIONAL
RIVER & RECREATION AREA
http://www.nps.gov/biso/

CUMBERLAND GAP NATIONAL
HISTORIC PARK
http://www.nps.gov/cuga/

TRAIL OF TEARS
NATIONAL HISTORIC TRAIL
http://www.nps.gov/trte/

MAMMOTH CAVE
NATIONAL PARK
http://www.nps.gov/maca/

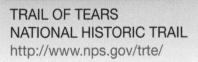

State Parks, Resorts & Historic Sites

Barren River Lake State Resort Park
(270) 646-2151, (800) 325-0057
parks.ky.gov/resortparks/br/

Ben Hawes State Park
(270) 684-9808
parks.ky.gov/stateparks/bh/

Big Bone Lick State Park
(859) 384-3522
parks.ky.gov/stateparks/bb/

**Blue Licks Battlefield
State Resort Park**
(800) 443-7008, (606) 298-5507
parks.ky.gov/resortparks/bl/

Boone Station State Historic Site
(859) 527-3131
parks.ky.gov/statehistoricsites/bs/

Buckhorn Lake State Resort Park
(800) 325-0058, (606) 398-7510
parks.ky.gov/resortparks/bk/

Carr Creek State Park
(606) 642-4050
parks.ky.gov/stateparks/ck/

Carter Caves State Resort Park
(800) 325-0059, (606) 286-4411
parks.ky.gov/resortparks/cc/

**Columbus-Belmont Battlefield
State Park**
(270) 677-2327
parks.ky.gov/stateparks/cb/

**Constitution Square
State Historic Site**
(859) 239-7089
parks.ky.gov/statehistoricsites/cs/

Cumberland Falls State Resort Park
(800) 325-0063, (606) 528-4121
parks.ky.gov/resortparks/cf/

Dale Hollow State Resort Park
(800) 325-2282, (270) 433-7431
parks.ky.gov/resortparks/dh/

Dr Thomas Walker Historic Site
(606) 546-4400
parks.ky.gov/statehistoricsite/dt/

EP (Tom) Sawyer State Park
(502) 426-8950
parks.ky.gov/stateparks/ep/

Fishtrap Lake State Park
(606) 437-7496
parks.ky.gov/stateparks/ft/

Fort Boonesborough State Park
(859) 527-3131
parks.ky.gov/stateparks/fb/

General Burnside Island State Park
(606) 561-4104
parks.ky.gov/stateparks/ge/

General Butler State Resort Park
(866) 462-8853, 732-4384
parks.ky.gov/resortparks/gb/

Grayson Lake State Park
(606) 474-9727
parks.ky.gov/stateparks/gl/

Greenbo Lake State Resort Park
(800) 325-0083, (606) 473-7324
parks.ky.gov/resortparks/go/

Green River Lake State Park
(270) 465-8255
parks.ky.gov/stateparks/gr/

**Isaac Shelby Cemetery
State Historic Site**
(859) 239-7089
parks.ky.gov/statehistoricsites/is/

Jefferson Davis State Historic Site
(270) 886-1765
parks.ky.gov/statehistoricsites/jd/

Jenny Wiley State Resort Park
(800) 325-0142, (606) 886-2711
parks.ky.gov/resortparks/jw/

John James Audubon State Park
(270) 826-2247
parks.ky.gov/stateparks/au/

Kenlake State Resort Park
(800) 325-0143, (270) 474-2211
parks.ky.gov/resortparks/kl/

KY Dam Village State Resort Park
(800) 325-0146, (270) 362-4271
parks.ky.gov/resortparks/kd/

Kincaid Lake State Park
(859) 654-3531
parks.ky.gov/stateparks/kn/

Kingdom Come State Park
(606) 589-2479
parks.ky.gov/stateparks/kc/

Lake Barkley State Resort Park
(800) 325-1708, (270) 924-1131
parks.ky.gov/resortparks/lb/

Lake Cumberland State Resort Park
(800) 325-1709, (270) 343-3111
parks.ky.gov/resortparks/lc/

Lake Malone State Park
(270) 657-2111
parks.ky.gov/stateparks/lm/

Levi Jackson Wilderness Road
State Park
(606) 878-8000
parks.ky.gov/stateparks/lj/

Lincoln Homestead State Park
(859) 336-7461
parks.ky.gov/stateparks/lh/

Mineral Mound State Park
(270) 388-3673
parks.ky.gov/stateparks/mm/

My Old Kentucky Home State Park
(502) 348-3502
parks.ky.gov/stateparks/mk/

Natural Bridge State Resort Park
(800) 325-1710, (606) 663-2214
parks.ky.gov/resortparks/nb/

Nolin Lake State Park
(270) 286-4240
parks.ky.gov/stateparks/nl/

Old Fort Harrod State Park
(859) 734-3314
parks.ky.gov/stateparks/fh/

Old Mulkey Meetinghouse State
Historic Site
(270) 487-8481
parks.ky.gov/statehistoricsites/om/

Paintsville Lake State Park
(606) 297-8486
parks.ky.gov/stateparks/pl/

Pennyrile Forest State Resort Park
(800) 325-1711, (270) 797-3421
parks.ky.gov/resortparks/pf/

Perryville Battlefield
State Historic Site
(859) 332-8631
parks.ky.gov/statehistoricsites/pb/

Pine Mountain State Resort Park
(800) 325-1712, (606) 337-3066
parks.ky.gov/resortparks/pm/

Rough River Dam State Resort Park
(800) 325-1713, (270) 257-2311
parks.ky.gov/resortparks/rr/

Taylorsville Lake State Park
(502) 477-8713
parks.ky.gov/stateparks/tl/

Waveland State Historic Park
(859) 272-3611
parks.ky.gov/statehistoricsites/wv/

White Hall State Historic Site
(859) 623-9178
parks.ky.gov/statehistoricsites/wh/

Wickliff Mounds State Historic Site
(270) 335-3681
parks.ky.gov/statehistoricsites/wm/

William Whitley House
State Historic Site
(606) 355-2881
parks.ky.gov/statehistoricsites/ww/

Yatesville Lake State Park
(606) 673-1492
parks.ky.gov/stateparks/yl/

Paducah-McCracken County

Visit the studios and galleries of resident artists in the Lower Town Arts District

First time visitors to the Quilt Museum marvel at the artistry of the varied exhibits

Art, Rhythm & Rivers…feel the movement. Captivated by inspiring views and an art-friendly culture, artists from around the world are relocating to Paducah. They are moved by the unique variety of art forms in this vibrant river town.

The movement of Paducah's art, rhythm and rivers can be heard and seen at various venues throughout the historic downtown and Lower Town Arts District. Along brick sidewalks and tree lined streets, anchor attractions like the Museum of the American Quilters Society, the Carson Center for the Performing Arts, River Heritage Museum and others are all within walking distance. The downtown's beautiful 19th century architecture entices visitors to explore antiques and specialty shops, and one-of-a-kind eateries.

Visit the Lower Town Arts District, the result of Paducah's award winning, nationally recognized Artist Relocation Program. The district hosts extended hours (1-9 p.m.) and features hands-on demonstrations and musical entertainment on the "Second Saturday" gallery walk each month. Nearly 20 select galleries, cafés and artist studios welcome visitors seven days a week to this thriving neighborhood listed on the National Register of Historic Places.

The past comes alive in this historic hamlet where hospitality flows as freely as the nearby rivers. Sample the innovative cuisine while relaxing in casual elegance. Feel the movement…travel to Paducah.

128 Broadway
Paducah, KY 42001
(270) 443-8783
(800) PADUCAH (723-8224)

**Paducah Convention
& Visitors Bureau**

www.paducahtourism.org

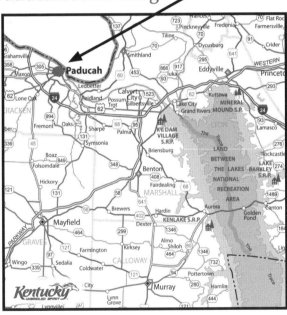

DIRECTIONS: Exits 4 & 11 off I-24. Follow signs for Downtown Loop

ADMISSION: Prices vary

HOURS: Museums, galleries, shops and restaurants host varied hours seven days a week. Contact Paducah CVB or visit www.paducahtourism.org for details

Patti's 1880s Settlement

Family dinner at Patti's

Patti's famous 2" pork chop dinner

Patti's 1880s Settlement is one of Western Kentucky's hidden treasures, home to Patti's 1880s Restaurant, which is famous for its two-inch thick charbroiled pork chops, mile high meringue pies, and fresh flowerpot bread. Patti's is located in the town of Grand Rivers at the northern entrance to the Land Between the Lakes.

Founded by Bill and Patti Tullar and family in 1977, Patti's started as Hamburger Patti's Ice Cream Parlor. From its small beginning, Patti's has evolved into a sprawling eatery serving 300,000 meals per year with nine log cabin gift shops, a dessert and coffee café, a miniature golf course, a rock climbing wall, and remote control coin operated boats.

Guests come from far and wide to enjoy Patti's great food, ambience and shopping. Patti's dining rooms are decorated with antiques, art, floral arrangements, lights, quilts and stained glass. Servers, attired in floral peasant dresses, bear pewter-plated meals piled high with hearty portions — tempting even the most discriminating taste buds.

The second Friday in November is the start of Patti's Holiday Festival of Lights. This festival (one of the finest holiday displays in western Kentucky) features 500,000 holiday lights twinkling throughout restaurants, shops and grounds.

A favorite of tour groups, family gatherings, prom and wedding parties, Patti's proudly displays honors received over the years. These honors include Southern Living magazine's first ever Readers' Choice Award for "Best Small Town Restaurant" in the southeastern U.S. (1997) and the "Top Restaurant for Tourism" by the state of Kentucky. In 2005 Patti's was named the No. 1 non-franchised restaurant by Kentucky Living Magazine.

Box 111 (Main Street)
Grand Rivers, KY 42045
(888) 736-2515 (270) 362-8844
pattis1880s@ccol.net

www.pattis-settlement.com

Patti's 1880s Settlement

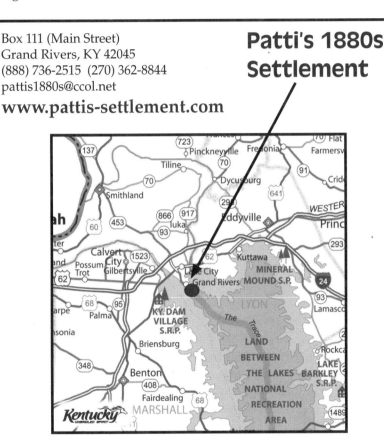

DIRECTIONS: Take US 60W to Bluegrass Pkwy; Take I-65 S to Western Kentucky Pkwy; Take I-24 to Exit 31; go south 453; take the first left; go 1/4 mile to the stop sign. Patti's 1880s Settlement will be on your left, our Iron Kettle on your right

HOURS: Patti's: Mon-Sun 10:30-8 (Jan-Mar); Mon-Sun 10:30-9 (Apr-Dec). Iron Kettle: Mon-Fri 10:30-7; Sat-Sun 10:30-8; Sunday Brunch 9:30. Gift Shops: 11-close. Call for special holiday hours

Prizer Point Marina & Resort

Prizer Point is surrounded by water on three sides and offers all of the amenities including "The Iceberg" for family fun

Prizer Point offers a great splash/ play/swim pool, pontoon boats with slides and lakefront lodging and camping

Every Good Memory has a Point...Prizer Point Marina & Resort

Prizer Point Marina & Resort is the Kentucky Lakes and the Land Between the Lakes area's newest resort. We invite you to experience 57 acres of Kentucky beauty surrounded on three sides by water, and the other by woods.

Prizer Point Marina & Resort, has Kentucky's highest rating and is now a top 40 U.S. rated campground.

Our lodging is new or refurbished, and is available waterfront or with a water view. Several are handicapped accessible.

Adults can relax at Prizer Point knowing their kids stay happy. Kids can hike and bike, climb an iceberg or our new magnetic wall, ride on a three-wheel or six-seater bike; play in the splash pool, the big pool or on the playground. They can play basketball, volleyball or soccer. Next, they can hit the game room, or the paddle boats and kayaks. If their parents come along they can take out a pontoon with a slide, or a deck boat with skis and a tube. The next stop can be mini-golf or fishing. Of course there is pizza and ice cream available in our floating restaurant and store. Wrap it up with a campfire, s'mores and a tuck-in from Mom.

Check with us for special fall activity weekends.

1777 Prizer Point Road
Cadiz, KY 42211
(270) 522-3762 (800) 548-2048
prizerpoint@prizerpoint.com
www.prizerpoint.com

Prizer Point
Marina & Resort

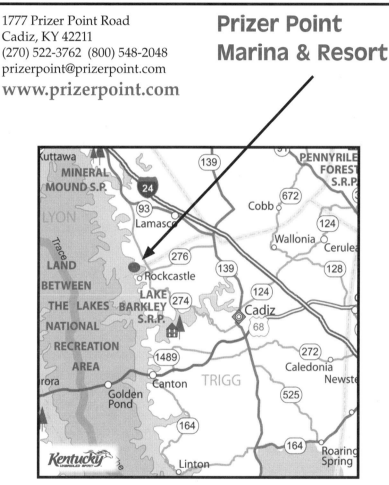

DIRECTIONS: Take US 60W to Bluegrass Pkwy; Take I-65 S to Western Kentucky Pkwy to I-24; From I-24 take Exit 56 and follow the signs

ADMISSION: Rates run $23-$300 per night

OPEN: Mar 15-Nov 6; closed Nov 7-Mar 2007

Trail of Tears National Historic Trail

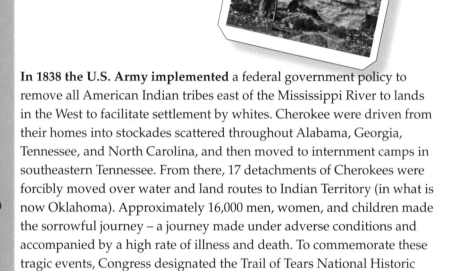

*Memorial to
Chief Whitepath and
Fly Smith*

In 1838 the U.S. Army implemented a federal government policy to remove all American Indian tribes east of the Mississippi River to lands in the West to facilitate settlement by whites. Cherokee were driven from their homes into stockades scattered throughout Alabama, Georgia, Tennessee, and North Carolina, and then moved to internment camps in southeastern Tennessee. From there, 17 detachments of Cherokees were forcibly moved over water and land routes to Indian Territory (in what is now Oklahoma). Approximately 16,000 men, women, and children made the sorrowful journey – a journey made under adverse conditions and accompanied by a high rate of illness and death. To commemorate these tragic events, Congress designated the Trail of Tears National Historic Trail in 1987.

Even though the Indian Removal Act of 1830 mandated the removal of all American Indian tribes and forced several southeastern tribes to move during the 1820s and 1830s, the congressionally designated trail is specific to the Cherokee experience.

The National Historic Trails System, established by the National Trails System Act of 1968, commemorates historic routes and promotes their preservation, and development for public use. National Historic Trails recognize diverse facets of history such as prominent past routes of exploration, migration, trade, communication and military action. The historic trails generally consist of remnant sites and trail segments, and thus are not necessarily contiguous. Although National Historic Trails are administered by federal agencies, land ownership may be in public or private hands. Today the trail includes about 2,200 miles of land and water routes, and traverses portions of nine states, including Kentucky.

2800 Ft. Campbell Blvd.
Hopkinsville, KY 42240
(270) 885-1499
**tourism@
visithopkinsville.com**

Trail of Tears Commemorative Park & Heritage Ctr.

DIRECTIONS: Take US 60W to Bluegrass Pkwy; Take I-65 S to Western Kentucky Pkwy; Take Edward Breathitt Pkwy; Located just off Edward Breathitt Pkwy (formerly Pennyrile Parkway,) Exit 8, Hwy 41 N

ADMISSION: Donations only

HOURS: The park is always open; Heritage Center open by appointment (270) 885-1499; Pow Wow Weekend, Sep 9-10, 2006

Hopkins County

Ruby Laffoon Cabin

Dawson Springs Museum & Art Center

Less than 200 miles from such major cities as Nashville, Louisville, Lexington, Paducah and Evansville, Hopkins County is the perfect one-tank weekend get-away. Filled with shopping, sports and entertainment your whole family is guaranteed to find something they love in one of Western Kentucky's most beautiful areas.

Things to see

Historic Hanson – Kentucky's Smallest Historic District; Western Kentucky Speedway-races April-October; Glema Mahr Center for the Arts–plays, music and workshops; Tradewater Canoe Livery–canoeing, camping and wildlife located near Pennyrile Forest State Resort Park; Downtown Dawson Springs – historical structures and museum, small town charm, shopping, dining and the fully restored Riverside Park (home to Tradewater Pirates baseball); Ruby Laffoon Cabin & Hopkins County Historical Society – one of Kentucky's most beloved governor's birthplace, memorabilia from the early 1800s; Downtown Madisonville – several blocks of enjoyment including a life-size facade of Montpelier, walking tours available upon request.

Hopkins County also boasts three superb golf courses, fishing, hunting, and breathtaking parks. You may also enjoy one of our yearly events: Hanson Mule Days, Mortons Gap Coal Field Festival, Party in the Park, Wait-A-Minute Festival in May, Dawson Springs Annual Bar-B-Q and Fireworks, Hopkins County Horse Show in July, "Hats Off to Hopkins County" in September, and Return To Bethlehem in December.

15 East Center Street
Madisonville, KY 42431
(270) 821-4171
hopkinstourism@charter.net

www.hopkinscountytourism.com

Hopkins County Tourist Commission

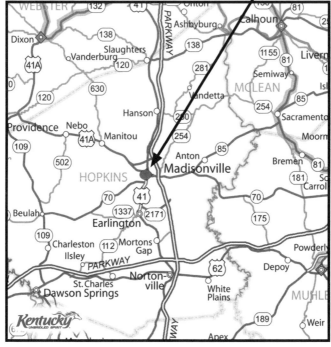

DIRECTIONS: To Madisonville: Take US 60W to Bluegrass Pkwy; Take I-65 S to Western Kentucky Pkwy; Take Edward Breathitt Pkwy (formerly Pennyrile Pkwy); Take Exits 37-44. To Historic Hanson: Take Exit 49. To Dawson Springs - Exit 24 off Wendell Ford Pkwy (formerly Western KY Pkwy)

ADMISSION: Prices vary, contact Tourist Commission for details

HOPKINS COUNTY - Bluegrass, Blues & Barbeque Region

Bluegrass & Barbeque

Find the roots of bluegrass music and the state's best barbecue in Owensboro. Bluegrass and Barbecue just go together, so plan your trip around a visit to the International Bluegrass Music Museum and dinner at the famous Moonlite Bar-B-Q Inn.

Things to see

Start your day by stepping back in time as you listen to original recordings of bluegrass artists, and watch bluegrass legends talk and perform on video at Owensboro's International Bluegrass Music Museum, the world's only facility dedicated to the international history and preservation of this popular style of music. Be sure to allow time to visit the interactive displays featuring photographs, music and memorabilia from the founders of this unique and exciting genre of music.

Eat dinner at the Moonlite Bar-B-Q Inn and you will taste why it was voted the best barbecue in Kentucky by both *Kentucky Monthly* and *Kentucky Living* magazines. People even call nationwide to have it shipped to their door. *Gourmet Magazine* notes, "Most of America's

serious barbecue scenes specialize in just one kind of meat, b[...]
Owensboro, at Moonlite, they've got it all and it's all good."[...]
taste their famous mutton, what the *L.A. Times calls* "Older, W[...]
Lamb," or go for the more traditional pork, beef or chicken. [...]
menu or choose the fabulous buffet – it will be a meal you won't forget.

Moonlite Bar-B-Q

2840 West Parrish Avenue
Owensboro, KY 42301
(800) 322-8989
www.moonlite.com

HOURS: Mon-Thu 9-9; Fri-Sat
9-9:30; Sun 10-3

BUFFET HOURS: Mon-Sat
11-2; Mon-Thu 4-9; Fri-Sat 3:30-
9:30; Sun 10-3

International Bluegrass Music Museum

207 East Second Street
Owensboro, KY 42303
(888) MY-BANJO
www.bluegrass-museum.org

ADMISSION: Seniors & Adults
$5; Students $2; 6 & under free;
Members free; group rates available

HOURS: Tue-Sat 10-5; Sun 1-4

Owensboro-Daviess County Tourist Commission

215 East Second Street • Owensboro, KY 42303 • (800) 489-1311

www.visitowensboro.com

ree Friday Night Concerts

Every Friday night this summer, there is free music on the Owensboro riverfront. Friday After 5 starts things off at 5 p.m. on the RiverPark Center stages. As the sun goes down, the music continues just a few blocks away at the Big E Sunset Series on the Owensboro Showcase Stage until 1 a.m. Enjoy both these free music festivals and all of the festivities overlooking the beautiful Ohio River.

Things to see

Friday After 5 began a decade ago to breathe new life into Owensboro's riverfront entertainment area after dark. RiverPark Center provides Friday After 5 a beautiful location with its spectacular, open-air terrace overlooking the Ohio River. The main stage is set up on the BB&T Plaza's east end using the decorative necklace-lighted Glover Cary Bridge as a backdrop. As the name suggests, the music begins after 5 p.m and wraps up at 10 p.m. Beer and wine are available for purchase on the terrace. Arts and crafts, and food vendors are set up along the riverfront, under the generous canopy of mature shade trees that line the Smothers Park setting. The event is family-friendly with games and a play structure for the kids.

The Big E Sunset Series extends the free music into the night at Owensboro's largest hotel, the Executive Inn Rivermont. Just a short walk takes you over to the equally impressive open-air Owensboro Showcase Stage located in Mitch McConnell Plaza. The hottest bands from throughout the region take the outdoor stage at 9 p.m. and continue until 1 a.m. On most Friday nights you'll see several boats anchored in the river with passengers kicked back and enjoying the entertainment. If you find yourself not wanting the evening to end you can always book a room at the hotel and take the elevator home.

Big E Sunset Series

Executive Inn Rivermont
One Executive Boulevard
Owensboro, KY 42301
(800) 626-1936
www.AtTheBigE.com

ADMISSION: Free

HOURS: Fri 9-1

DIRECTIONS: Downtown at St. Elizabeth & Veterans (First St.)

Friday After 5

RiverPark Cente
101 Daviess Street
Owensboro, KY 42301
(270) 687-2770
www.fridayafter5.com

ADMISSION: Free

HOURS: Fri 5-10

DIRECTIONS: Downtown at Daviess & Veterans (First St.)

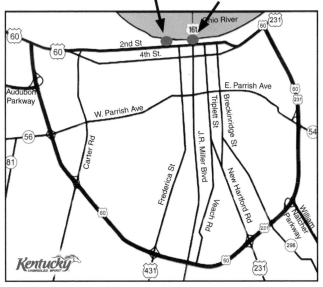

Owensboro-Daviess County Tourist Commission
215 East Second Street • Owensboro, KY 42303 • (800) 489-1311

www.visitowensboro.com

National Corvette Museum

Corvette engineering area

Award-winning design structure

The National Corvette Museum is a 68,000-square-foot tribute to America's Sports Car. Over 70 Corvettes are displayed throughout every curvaceous turn of the museum's extraordinary structure. Exhibits and displays inside the museum cover all Corvette model years, starting with the birth of Corvette in 1953 and going beyond the present to futuristic concept Corvettes. From nostalgic settings that stir memories and convey the history of this legendary automobile, to displays that focus on development and racing – the museum is an unforgettable experience. Sit behind the wheel of the latest Corvette as part of your tour experience and take a chance to win a new one.

See the only 1983 Corvette in existence; the newest Corvette model; exotic show cars that never made it to the showroom; unique race cars and watch a new Corvette owner take delivery inside the museum. Watch Corvette's history unfold in our 165-seat Chevrolet Theater and shop for unique Corvette collectibles and more in our 3,300-square-foot Corvette Store. Tours are self-guided and photography is welcome inside. April through October is the perfect time to be a part of the museum's many on-site events featuring exciting displays, seminars, celebrity car shows and more.

Located just minutes from the Corvette Assembly Plant, the museum is a true automotive tribute to the Corvette – in the heart of Corvette country. Come on in and imagine yourself behind the wheel.

350 Corvette Drive
Bowling Green, KY 42101
(270) 781-7973 (800) 53-VETTE
www.corvettemuseum.com

National Corvette Museum

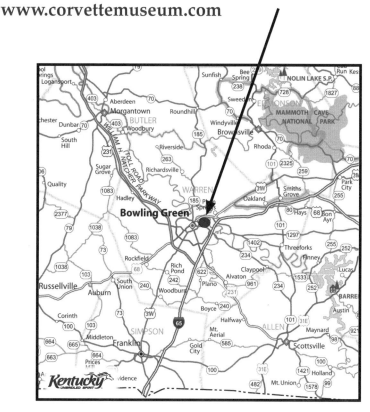

DIRECTIONS: Take US 60W to Bluegrass Pkwy; Take I-65 S; From I-65 take Exit 28; take a left at the first light; the museum is on the right

ADMISSION: Adults $8; Children $4.50; Seniors $6; Family rate $20; discounts available for AAA members and military personnel

HOURS: Open daily 8-5 (Central Time); Closed Easter, Thanksgiving, Christmas Eve, Christmas Day and New Year's Day

WARREN COUNTY - Caves, Lakes & Corvettes Region

Kentucky Library & Museum

1815 Log House

Gallery Opening

Opening its doors in 1939, the Kentucky Library & Museum's mission is to enhance an understanding of Kentucky and its people. Housed in the National Register Kentucky Building, KYL&M collects art and artifacts, documents and photographs, rare books and anything else that can help explain Kentucky, past and present.

The research library holds one of the largest genealogical collections in the state, as well as the largest collection of Civil War and southern history documents on microforms in the entire South. One-of-a-kind documents, historic photographs, out-of-print and rare books make up the library's collections.

The museum collects anything and everything connected to Kentucky. From modern art to rare silver, Kentucky-made furniture to WKU football uniforms, the museum creates exciting exhibits on a wide range of topics using its outstanding collections. We are well known for our quilt collection, several of which just returned from a tour in Europe.

KYL&M operates the 1815 Log House, next door to the Kentucky Building, restored and furnished to show how a wealthy family lived in this region at the end of the frontier period.

Workshops, lectures, hands-on programs, events and art camps provide visitors with opportunities to learn and improve their skills in papermaking, painting, basket-making, open-hearth cooking or learning how to trace their roots. Special events such as gallery openings, appraisal days, receptions and art shows are open to the public.

1906 College Heights Boulevard
Bowling Green, KY 42101
(270) 745-2592
kymus@wku.edu

www.wku.edu/library/kylm

Kentucky Library & Museum

DIRECTIONS: Take US 60W to Bluegrass Pkwy; Take I-65 S; From I-65; take Exit 28 to Bowling Green; Follow 31-W South and Hwy 68-80 (Adams St.) to Western Kentucky University; Just past 14th Street, look for the directional sign to the Kentucky Library & Museum and turn left

ADMISSION: Adults $5; Seniors & children $2.50; Family $10; Members free. Group rates by reservation

HOURS: Gallery hours Mon-Sat 9-4; Sun 1-4. Office hours Mon-Fri 8-4:30

Mammoth Cave National Park

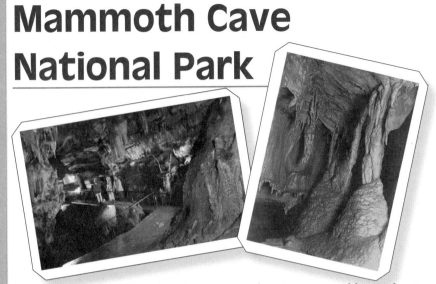

Mammoth Cave National Park is a great place to come and learn about caves, forests, groundwater, wildlife, and history.

Nestled into the gentle rolling hills of central Kentucky, Cave Country offers year-round natural beauty in Mammoth Cave National Park and nearby show-caves. Mammoth Cave National Park protects over 360 miles of cave passages and over 52,000 above-ground acres of scenic forests, streams, sinkholes, ponds, meadows, and more. Only about 10 miles of the cave are shown to the public in 11 separate tours that vary in length, times, and costs. Mammoth Cave National Park has nearly 80 miles of trails, which wander, through forests, along rivers, past sinkholes, and through historic areas. Sloan's Crossing Pond Trail and the Heritage Trail are both accessible to those with mobility impairments. On the Historic Tour of Mammoth Cave, visitors pass through Mammoth Dome, a 192-foot high shaft with water constantly dripping down into it. About 30 feet above that dome is Mammoth Dome Sink. Visit here before or after the Historic Tour to connect the sinkhole and the disappearing streams near it to what you see in the cave. Down the trail to Echo River Spring, see all the features of a karst landscape (sinkholes, disappearing streams, caves, and springs).

About a half mile from the Visitor Center is Dixon Cave, speculated to have once been a part of Mammoth Cave, separated by the cave-in that created the Historic Entrance. Today it is closed to the public, but is an important hibernacula for bats and a good example of a large sinkhole. Slide shows and boat rides are available.

PO Box 7
Mammoth Cave, KY 42259
(270) 758-2180

www.nps.gov/maca

Mammoth Cave National Park

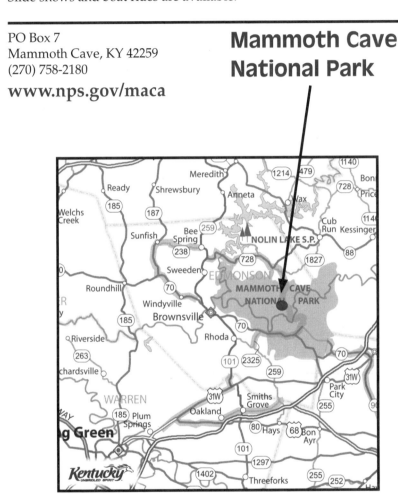

DIRECTIONS: Take US 60W to Bluegrass Pkwy; Take I-65 S; From North I-65 take Exit 53 (Cave City), turn right (west) to Park entrance; from South I-65 take Exit 48 (Park City), turn left to Park entrance

ADMISSION: Park admission is free; cave tour fees vary

HOURS: Open 24-7, year round. Closed Christmas Day. Interpretive tours available throughout the day

Somerset-Pulaski County

"Come jump in our lake!"

Picturesque Lake Cumberland

Located in South Central Kentucky just minutes off I-75, Pulaski County is nestled between the Daniel Boone National Forest and Lake Cumberland. Somerset-Pulaski County, the "Gateway to Lake Cumberland," attracts more than 1.5 million visitors each year. With over "1,255 miles of possibilities," Lake Cumberland has something for everyone!

Things to see

Lake Cumberland, one of the largest, man-made lakes in the nation, was formed in the 1940s by damming a large section of the Cumberland River. Today, the 1,255 miles of Lake Cumberland shoreline supports over 63,000 acres of water. A favorite destination for outdoor and water sports enthusiasts, Lake Cumberland is the perfect location for a weekend getaway, vacation or group outing, providing great accommodations and dining.

In addition to all that the lake offers, there is so much more to see and do in Somerset-Pulaksi County. From antiquing and flea markets, classic cars and guided Civil War Battlefield tours, to festivals and concerts, you will discover as much fun off the lake as on.

522 Ogden Street
Somerset, KY 42501
(606) 679-6394 (800) 642-6287
www.lakecumberland.com

Somerset-Pulaski Tourism

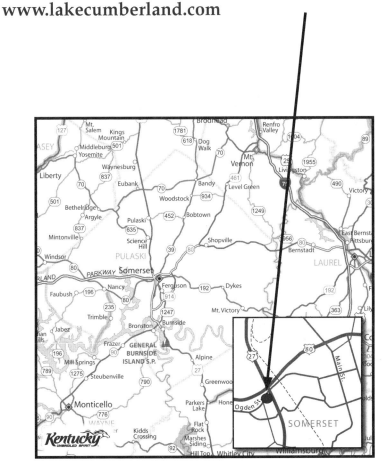

DIRECTIONS: Take I-75S; Take Exit 62; US 25 towards Mt. Vernon; turns into 461; Turn Right on Hwy 80; Turn Left Ogden

ADMISSION: Prices vary, contact Tourism Office for details

Big South Fork Scenic Railway

Big South Fork Engine #105

McCreary County Museum

Take a relaxing ride back in time where modern day headaches disappear. You'll find something the whole family can enjoy – history, nature, music and so much more.

The Big South Fork Scenic Railway begins its journey in the historic company town of Stearns. Stearns served as the operational hub for the Stearns Coal and Lumber Company. The train travels upon the old Kentucky & Tennessee Railway making its way into the gorge of the Big South Fork National River & Recreation Area. The 256-foot tunnel acts as a portal into the past as visitors follow along mountain streams and pass through lush vegetation with a host of hardwood and evergreen trees. Each gentle curve along the railway reveals a spectacular scenic view or evidence of life from days gone by before reaching your stop at the coal mining camp of Blue Heron. The camp is operated by the National Park Service as an outdoor interpretive center, but the audio recordings of the people who lived and worked here keep its spirit alive.

Your ticket admission includes visitation to the McCreary County Museum. The museum is within walking distance of the depot as well as a number of gift and craft shops. Regular excursions are April through

October with special trains running for Halloween and Christmas. For more information on the Big South Fork Scenic Railway, call 800-462-5664 or visit our website www.bsfsry.com.

---

100 Henderson Street
Stearns, KY 42647
(800) 462-5664
info@bsfsry.com
www.bsfsry.com

Big South Fork Scenic Railway

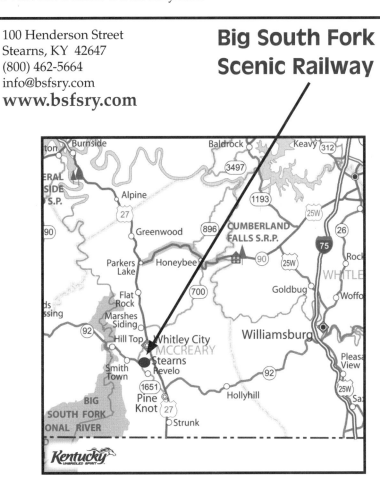

DIRECTIONS: Take I-75S; Take Hwy 92; From U.S. 27 turn onto Hwy 92 West; Travel one mile and turn right onto Hwy 1651 into downtown Stearns

ADMISSION: Adults $15; Seniors (60+) $14; Children (age 3-12) $7.50

HOURS: Apr: Thu-Fri 11, Sat 11 and 2:30; May-Sep: Wed-Fri 11, Sat-Sun 11 and 2:30; Oct: Tue-Fri 11; Sat-Sun 11 and 2:30; Nov: First two Saturdays 11 and 2:30

Big South Fork National Park-McCreary County

MCCREARY COUNTY - Southern Lakes & Rivers Region

Located in southeastern Kentucky and northeastern Tennessee, the free-flowing Big South Fork of the Cumberland River and its tributaries pass through 90 miles of scenic gorges and valleys containing a wide range of natural and historic features. The 125,310-acre area offers a broad range of recreational opportunities including camping, whitewater rafting, kayaking, canoeing, hiking, horseback riding, mountain biking, hunting and fishing.

There are two Visitor Centers including the Park Headquarters at Bandy Creek Visitor Center in Tennessee and the Stearns Depot Visitor Center (located in downtown Stearns, 1 ½ mile west off Hwy 27 on KY 92, in the Big South Fork Scenic Railway Depot, open April-October 9:30 a.m. - 4:30 p.m.). The Blue Heron Mining Community Museum, located nine miles west of Stearns, on Hwy 742 is open all year.

The U.S. Army Corps of Engineers, with its experience in managing river basins, was charged with land acquisition, planning and development of facilities. Now completed, these lands and facilities are operated and maintained by the National Park Service for the benefit and use of the public.

Stearns Depot Visitor Center
100 Henderson Street
Stearns, KY 42647
(800) 462-5664

www.nps.gov

Big South Fork
National Park

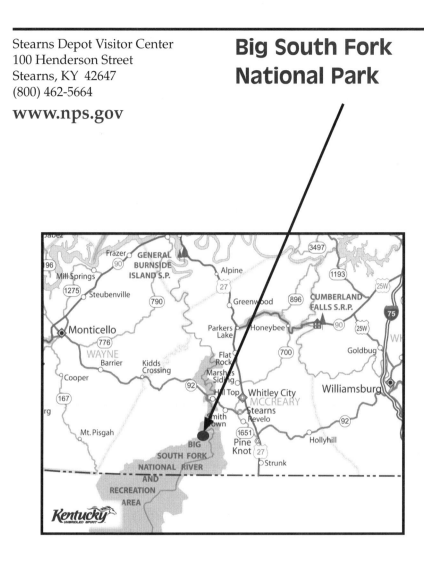

DIRECTIONS: Take I-75S. Take Hwy 92. From U.S. 27 turn onto Hwy 92 West. Travel one mile and turn right onto Hwy 1651 into downtown Stearns

HOURS: The park is open year round; the Kentucky Visitor Center is open daily from May-Oct 9-5:30; Nov-Apr hours vary, call ahead for details

MCCREARY COUNTY - Southern Lakes & Rivers Region

Abraham Lincoln Birthplace National Historic Site

The farm Thomas Lincoln and his wife Nancy moved to in the fall of 1808 was just within the borders of "the Barrens," a 400-square-mile subregion of the Pennyroyal that Native Americans had burned repeatedly to create grazing land for game. Tall grasses dominated the Barrens, with scattered trees present only along stream courses. Locally known as the Sinking Spring Farm, the Lincoln property contained a large spring that emerged from a rock ledge and flowed through a limestone channel, dropped into a deep sinkhole and disappeared into the earth.

On high ground close to the spring, the elder Lincoln constructed a one-room log cabin, where his son Abraham (16th president of the United States) was born on February 12, 1809. The young Lincoln lived on the Sinking Spring Farm for only two years; in 1811, after a legal dispute centering on land patents, the Lincolns moved to a 230-acre farm on Knob Creek, approximately 10 miles northeast.

Abraham Lincoln Birthplace National Historic Site (established by Congress on July 17, 1916) contains 116.5 acres, representing approximately one-third of the original 348.5-acre Lincoln farm along the South Fork of Nolin Creek. The Beaux-Arts classical granite and marble Memorial Building containing the traditional Lincoln birth cabin sits on a

knoll adjacent to the Sinking Spring. Roughly triangular in shape, the site is located in the rolling hill country of Larue County, three miles south of Hodgenville, the county seat, and approximately 50 miles south of Louisville. U.S. 31E/Hwy 61 bisects the Site on a north-south axis.

Abraham Lincoln Boyhood Home at Knob Creek became a part of the park in 2001 and is located 10 miles northeast of the birthplace on US 31E.

2995 Lincoln Farm Road
Hodgenville, KY 42748
(270) 358-3137
www.nps.gov/abli/

Abraham Lincoln Birthplace National Historic Site

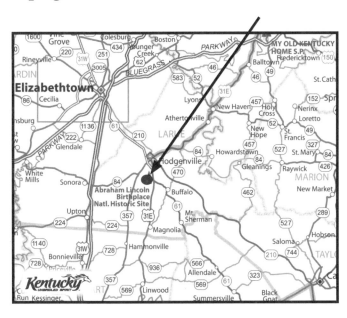

LARUE COUNTY - Kentucky Derby Region

DIRECTIONS: Take US 60W to Bluegrass Pkwy; Take U.S. 31E. The park picnic area and additional hiking trails are located across U.S. 31E and KY 61 from the visitor center.

HOURS: Memorial Day-Labor Day: 8-6:45; the remainder of the year: 8-4:45; Boyhood Home: daylight hours year around; interpretive staff Apr 1-Oct 31

Kentucky Railway Museum

A visit to the Kentucky Railway Museum in New Haven offers a rare glimpse at small town America at its best! Visitors can recapture the romance of the local passenger train when rail travel offered small town America a link to the rest of the world.

The Kentucky Railway Museum owes its beginning to a small number of rail enthusiasts who formed a local chapter of the National Railway Historical Society in 1948. Today the steam locomotive that started it all — the L&N 152 — still brings goose bumps when the whistle sounds just as it did in those long ago days.

What to see

Enjoy a 22-mile train excursion through the scenic and historic Rolling Fork River Valley on a restored passenger train. For a unique dining experience, our dinner train recreates the rail dining service of the 1940s. A delicious meal and excellent service await you. Visit the museum's model train facility and its collection of railroad artifacts and memorabilia — all housed in a replica of the original New Haven Depot. Exhibits from a variety of time periods include a dining car, handcar, track inspection car, steam locomotive whistles and a ticket office, plus much more.

Much more than a museum, the Kentucky Railway Museum offers unique special train excursions and events including the Mystery Theatre, Dinner Trains, Train Robbery, Day Out With Thomas and Easter, Halloween and Christmas Trains.

136 South Main Street
New Haven, KY 40051
(800) 272-0152

www.kyrail.org

Kentucky Railway Museum

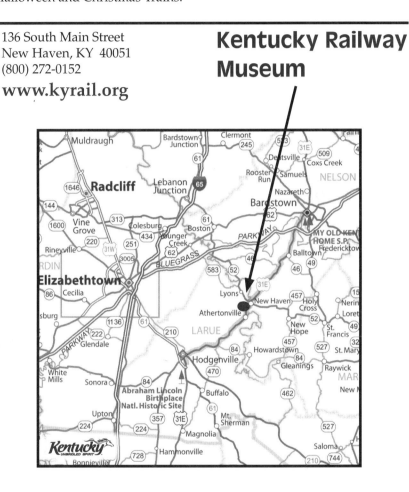

DIRECTIONS: Take U.S. 60 W to Bluegrass Pkwy. Take Exit 21 to U.S. 31 E

ADMISSION: Museum only: Adults $4; Children (2-12) $2; Train fare including museum: Adults $15; Children $10. Please call for special event pricing

HOURS: Museum open all year 10-4; closed Sun-Mon during Jan-Mar

NELSON COUNTY - Kentucky Derby Region

Bardstown-Nelson County

Heaven Hill Distilleries

Stephen Foster - The Musical

Nestled in the heart of Kentucky's rolling hills, Bardstown is a community that is strong in spirit. A Southern spirit that welcomes you home to one of "The Best Small Towns" in America. A religious spirit that's appropriate for the home of the first diocese of the West. And a little spirit called bourbon.

Eclectic shops, cultural and historical heritage blend beautifully with that spirit. Visit My Old Kentucky Home State Park and Stephen Foster-The Musical, vintage trains, and museums dedicated to the Civil War, railroads and bourbon.

More than 30 annual events, including the Kentucky Bourbon Festival, welcome visitors from across the globe. Come sample the spirits, sounds and flavors that are quintessentially Bardstown.

Things to see
Abbey of Gethsemani; Around the Town Carriage; Bardstown Historical Museum; Basilica of St. Joseph Proto-Cathedral; Civil War Museum of the Western Theatre and Museum Row at Old Bardstown Village;

Heaven Hill Distilleries Bourbon Heritage Center and Trolley; Horizon Hopper Adventures; Jim Beam Outpost; Kentucky Railway Museum; Maker's Mark Distillery; My Old Kentucky Dinner Train; My Old Kentucky Home State Park; Old County Jail; Old Talbott Tavern; Oscar Getz Museum of Whiskey History; Sisters of Charity of Nazareth; Springhill Winery; Stephen Foster-The Musical; and Wickland.

One Court Square
Bardstown, KY 40004
(800) 638-4877 (502) 348-4877
info@bardstowntourism.com

Bardstown-Nelson County Tourism

www.visitbardstown.com

DIRECTIONS: From the Bluegrass Parkway take Exit 21 or 25. From I-65 take Exit 112 and travel about 15 miles east

ADMISSION: Call the Welcome Center for attraction pricing

HOURS: Welcome Center is open daily year-round; closed Sun-Mon Jan-Mar, Sun in Apr, Thanksgiving, Christmas Day and New Year's Day

NELSON COUNTY - Kentucky Derby Region

Lebanon-Marion County

Statue of Union General George H Thomas

Maker's Mark Distillery

The geographic center of the state, Lebanon is the true "Heart of Kentucky." With its non-stop activity and close proximity to larger cities, this community has preserved its small town way of life and peaceful rural qualities, just the right mix for a great getaway. Civil War and religious heritage permeate Lebanon and things get lively when Marion County Country Ham Days is celebrated downtown. The Live in Lebanon Concert Series reminds folks of the golden days of entertainment when Club 68 and Club Cherry regularly showcased famous acts.

Things to see

Take a free tour at world famous Maker's Mark Distillery. Visit Historic Penn's Store for a step back in time. Enjoy the self-guided "Confederate Gen. John Hunt Morgan in Lebanon" and "Historic Homes & Landmarks of Lebanon" walking/driving tours. The Centre Square Arts & Culture Center offers performing arts and a history museum; Graham Memorial Park features the Lebanon Aquatic Center with an indoor pool and 100-foot winding water slide.

Fagan Branch Reservoir and the Scott's Ridge Lookout are just two natural beauties that will take your breath away and there are family events almost every weekend. Enjoy eclectic dining in the beautiful, historic downtown then visit a horse farm or watch standardbreds warming up at the fairgrounds. Come feel the beat in the true "Heart of Kentucky."

239 North Spalding Avenue
Suite 200
Lebanon, KY 40033-1518
(270) 692-0021
visitlebanonky@alltel.net

www.visitlebanonky.com

Lebanon Tourist & Convention Commission

DIRECTIONS: Take US 60W to Bluegrass Pkwy; Take exit 42 to Hwy 555 turns into Hwy 55. Lebanon can be reached via Historic Hwy 68 from east to west and Hwys 55 & 49 from north to south

ADMISSION: Prices vary, call Tourism Office for details

HOURS: Open Mon-Fri 8-5

MARION COUNTY - Kentucky Derby Region

Shepherdsville-Bullitt County

Jim Beam American Outpost

Canoeing the Salt River

In Bullitt County we have the **Jim Beam American Outpost**, museum house and distillery. This 200-year-old landmark features the fascinating art of bourbon making as well as the Beam family history. From moonshine to modern manufacturing, you will get a new appreciation for our nation's only native spirit. Hey! You can even try a sip.

Bullitt County is also the home to **Bernheim Arboretum and Research Forest**. While at Bernheim, check out the Legends and Lore Trail. On this trail you will hear many stories about different trees including the Serviceberry Tree. It was so named because it is the first tree to bloom in Kentucky. These blooms would let the preachers know they could get about the hills and hollows to perform services that the winter freeze had kept them from.

Things to see

Canoeing the Class 1 Salt River can be great fun with the family or friends. The Salt River is a slow but steady flowing river with beautiful scenery (unless it has rained!). Choose the 11, 8, or 6-mile runs or the overnight 26-mile run.

Hawks View Gallery offers visitors a tour to see how artisans make handblown glass artwork on a large scale. Just off I-65 at Exit 121 you can tour, shop and enjoy a light lunch at the newly opened café.

You can also get your motor running at **Kart Kountry**. Chronological age makes no difference on the nation's longest go cart track. Add their newly remodeled putt putt course and you have the makings for an evening you won't soon forget.

395 Paroquet Springs Drive
Shepherdsville, KY 40165-0520
(800) 526-2068

www.travelbullitt.org

Shepherdsville-Bullitt County Tourism ·

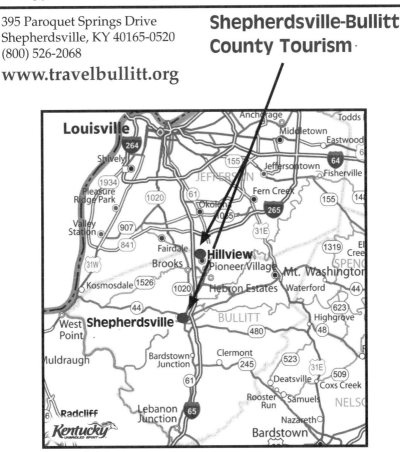

DIRECTIONS: Take I-65W to I-265S; Take I-65-S; Located right off I-65, just south of Louisville

ADMISSION: Prices free to varied, contact Tourism Office for details

Frazier International History Museum

Interpreter interacting with guests

18th Century small sword

Sitting proudly at the corner of Ninth and Main Streets in Louisville is a virtual powerhouse of diverse and dynamic history…a place where important stories are told by the people who lived them. When you visit you will embark on a journey spanning more than 1,000 years, including plenty of hands-on fun and state-of-the-art multimedia presentations. You will discover new things about world history, and about your own.

The Frazier is home to the world-class Frazier Arms Collection; a collection of artifacts covering four centuries including a flintlock attributed to George Washington, Teddy Roosevelt's "Big Stick" hunting rifle and artifacts from such 19th century notables as "Buffalo Bill" Cody and the outlaw Jesse James.

The Frazier is also home to The Royal Armouries USA, the only national museum collection represented outside Great Britain and including artifacts from the 11th to 20th centuries. From arrows to armor, the Royal Armouries galleries provide an in-depth look at British and European history and capture the art and artistry of early arms making.

The Frazier Education and Interpretive Center brings history to life every day through exciting performances by costumed interpreters. Each interpretation provides guests with a glimpse into a historical character's life.

829 West Main Street
Louisville, KY 40202
(502) 412-2280
info@fraziermuseum.org

www.fraziermuseum.org

Frazier International
History Museum

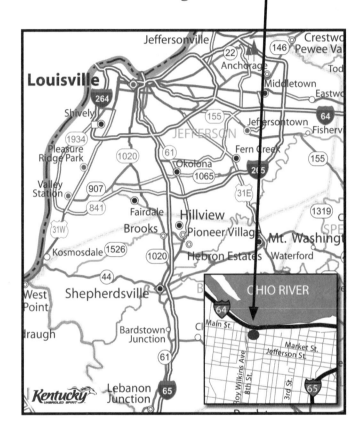

DIRECTIONS: The Frazier Museum is located at the corner of Ninth and Main Streets in downtown Louisville. Easily accessible from I-65, I-65 and I-71

ADMISSION: With audio tour: Adults $12; Seniors (60+) $10; Children under 14 $9; Children under 5 free (without audio tour). Special group rates available

HOURS: Mon-Sat 9-5; Sun 12-5; closed Thanksgiving Day and Christmas Day

JEFFERSON COUNTY - Kentucky Derby Region

Historic Locust Grove

Locust Grove, circa 1790, tells the story of builders William and Lucy Clark Croghan, the enslaved African-Americans who worked on the property, and Revolutionary War hero General George Rogers Clark. Clark captured the Northwest Territory from the British in 1779 and resided at Locust Grove with his sister and her family during the last years of his life. Their youngest brother William Clark and exploring partner Meriwether Lewis were entertained at Locust Grove upon returning from the Pacific. Today the 55 rolling acres include the restored Georgian house and dependencies exhibiting excellent examples of early American furniture and arts. Period-style gardens with rare and historic plants complement the landscape of woods and meadows. The Visitors Center houses exhibits, audio-visual presentations and the museum store. Located just six miles up river from Louisville, this National Historic Landmark is a unique example of early Kentucky architecture, craftsmanship and history.

Calendar of Events

Jun 25 & Sep 24 Antiques Market, 100 dealers, 10-4:30 (general admission); July 9 Slave Wedding, 6 pm (free); Oct 28-29 18th c. Market Fair, 10-4 (general admission); Nov 5 Lewis & Clark Homecoming Reenactment, 2 pm (free); Dec 8-9 Holiday Candlelight Tours 5:30-9 (general admission.) See our website for up-to-date program information.

561 Blankenbaker Lane
Louisville, KY 40207
(502) 897- 9845
lghh@locustgrove.org
www.locustgrove.org

Historic Locust Grove

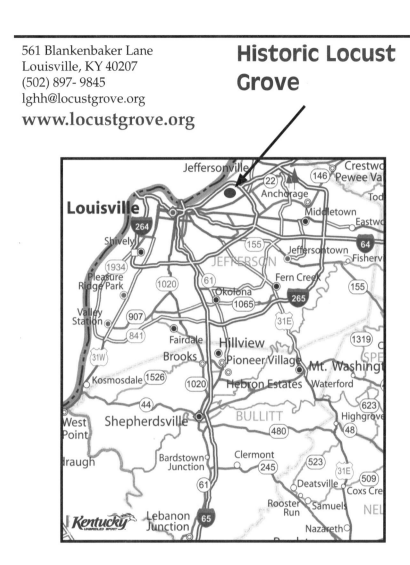

DIRECTIONS: Take I-64E to Louisville; From I-65 take I-71 N. Pass the I-64 split, exit Zorn Ave. Turn left. Turn right onto River Rd. Turn right onto Blankenbaker Ln. Proceed uphill, entrance to the Locust Grove parking lot on left. See our website for a map and complete directions

ADMISSION: Adults $6; Seniors $5; Children 6-12 $3

HOURS: 10-4:30 Mon-Sat; 1-4:30 Sun (last tour begins at 3:30); closed on New Year's Eve & New Year's Day, Easter, Derby Day, Thanksgiving, Christmas Eve & Christmas Day

Kentucky Derby Museum

The Kentucky Derby Museum captures the tradition and excitement of "the greatest two minutes in sports," the Kentucky Derby. The Kentucky Derby Museum is full of the sounds, images and artifacts that bring the pageantry and excitement of the Kentucky Derby to life for all of our visitors. Exhibits include high-tech computerized hands-on displays and video graphics.

Things to see

View "The Greatest Race," our 360-degree award winning video that is alive with the excitement of the crowds and the thunder of hoofs. Enjoy two floors of exhibits. Watch your favorite Derby on the Warner L. Jones Time Machine. Watch and listen while owners and trainers share their Derby stories. Listen to jockeys relive their Derby moments. Learn about the importance of African American jockeys and trainers. Take a guided walking tour of Churchill Downs, view the Grandstand, the Finish Line and Winner's Circle as our guide tours you through historical Churchill Downs. Visit our resident Thoroughbred and his companion, a miniature horse. Shop the Finish Line Gift Shop with its unique selection of equine-related gifts. Join us for a Backstretch Breakfast Tour where your group will savor the exclusive atmosphere of a morning at the track, watching the magical process of the thoroughbred's training workouts. We welcome you to the Kentucky Derby Museum where technology and history race together.

704 Central Avenue
Louisville, KY 40208
(502) 637-7097
info@derbymuseum.org
www.derbymuseum.org

Kentucky Derby Museum

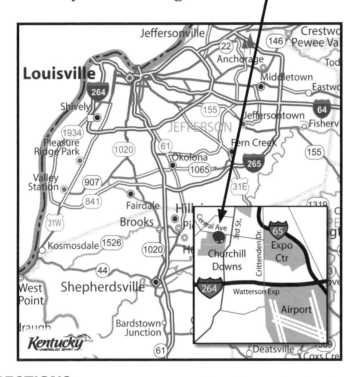

DIRECTIONS: Take I-64E to Louisville; Take I-65 South; take Exit 132 (Crittenden Drive). Go to the first light and turn right onto Central Ave.; the Kentucky Derby Museum is 1 mile down on the left

ADMISSION: Adults $9; Seniors $8; Children (5-12) $4; Children (4 and under) free

HOURS: Mon-Sat 8-5; Sun noon-5; closed on Thanksgiving Day, Christmas Day, Derby Day and Oaks Day (first Saturday in May and the preceding Friday) and Breeders' Cup Day when held in Louisville

Louisville Zoo

*Western lowland Gorilla Mshindi
Photo by Carol Weerts*

*King Louie, the rare white alligator
Photo by C. Jerry Abraham*

Enjoy wild adventures year round at the Louisville Zoo! Located in the heart of Louisville in the midst of a botanical garden setting, the Zoo is home to over 1,300 exotic animals.

Favorite exhibits include the award-winning Gorilla Forest, featuring pygmy hippos and 11 western lowland gorillas and the Islands Exhibit and Pavilion with playful orangutans, tigers, tapir, penguins, rare Island birds and more. The Herp Aquarium with its wide variety of reptiles, amphibians and fish is also home to vampire bats and a rare white alligator. And, the colorful, friendly birds in the new Lorikeet Landing are just waiting to eat nectar out of your hand.

Families love riding the miniature train or antique carousel, visiting the Boma petting zoo and relaxing while the youngsters play at the Outpost or Billabong playgrounds. Special events are scheduled throughout the year and education camps and classes are available for all ages.

The African Outpost Restaurant offers delicious meals; tasty snacks are available at concession stands throughout the Zoo. Visit our gift shops for truly unique zoovenirs. The Louisville Zoo – it's where the wild times are!

1100 Trevilian Way
Louisville, KY 40213
(502) 459-2181

Louisville Zoo

www.louisvillezoo.org

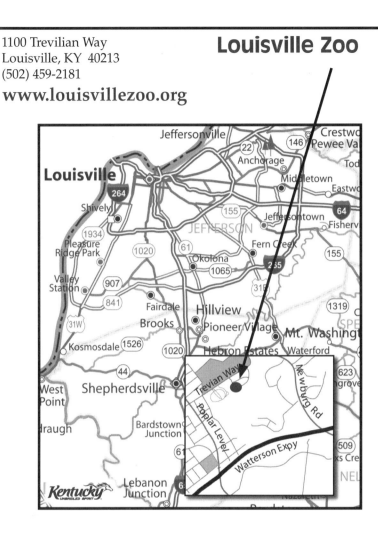

DIRECTIONS: From I-64 or I-71 take I-264 (Watterson Expressway) west to Exit 14 (Poplar Level Rd). Travel north on Poplar Level following the Zoo signs to 1100 Trevilian Way; from I-65 take I-264 east

ADMISSION: Adults (12-59) $10.95; Children (3-11) $7.95; Seniors (60+) $8.95; Infants and Zoo Members free. Group Rates are available for parties of 20 or more. Certain events require a specially priced ticket. Rates subject to change

HOURS: Sep-Mar 10-4; Apr-Labor Day 10-5; closed Thanksgiving Day, Christmas Day and New Year's Day. Call for summer evening hours

Muhammad Ali Center

*Muhammad Ali photo by John Lair
and Ali Center photos courtesy of the
Muhammad Ali Center*

The Muhammad Ali Center is both a destination site and an international education and communications center inspired by the ideals of its founder Muhammad Ali. The Ali Center's innovative exhibits, educational and public programming and global initiatives carry on Muhammad's legacy and inspire exploration of the greatness within ourselves.

Things to see

Two-and-a-half levels of interactive exhibits and multimedia presentations tell Ali's story through six core values of his life: *respect, confidence, conviction, dedication, spirituality* and *giving*. Enjoy learning about Ali's Louisville roots, unprecedented boxing career, his societal and religious convictions and global humanitarianism. Experience interactive boxing fun in *Train With Ali* and explore your own character strengths in *Walk With Ali*. Be sure to visit the global collection of children's artwork beautifully displayed in the *Hope and Dream* exhibit. Finish up your tour with two changing exhibit galleries, the Howard L. Bingham Gallery and LeRoy Neiman Gallery.

Find a variety of products in the Ali Center Store including *Ali by Adidas* apparel, crafts and collectibles from around the world, books, DVDs, CDs, souvenirs and more. The Ali Center also includes a video-on-demand area of Ali's most memorable fights and a library and archives.

JEFFERSON COUNTY - Kentucky Derby Region

One Muhammad Ali Plaza
144 North Sixth Street
Louisville, KY 40202
(502) 584-9254

Muhammad Ali Center

www.alicenter.org

DIRECTIONS: From I-64 West: Exit on 3rd Street/River Rd. (Exit 5B), right on River Road, left on 6th Street, entrance one-half block on right. From I-71 and I-65: Take I-64 West. Exit on 3rd Street/River Rd. (Exit 5B), right on River Road, left on 6th Street, entrance one-half block on right. From I-64 East: Cross the Sherman Minton Bridge. Exit on 9th Street. (Exit 4), left on Market and left on 5th Street. Left on Main Street and right on 6th Street, entrance one-half block on left

ADMISSION: Adults $9; Seniors (65+) $8; Students with ID $5; Children (6-12) $4; Groups (20+) $7, free for members and children 5 and under

HOURS: Open Mon-Sat 9:30-5; Sun noon-5; Closed New Year's Day, Easter Sunday, Independence Day, Thanksgiving Day and Christmas Day. Open Kentucky Derby Day 9:30-1

St. James Court Art Show

St. James Court Fountain

A top 20 Southeast Tourism Event

Held annually the first weekend in October since 1956 the St. James Court Art Show began with a few pieces of art hung on a clothesline between two trees. The $150 in sales for the day was divided among 15 artists.

A lot can change in 50 years. This year's art show will spill out into five Old Louisville neighborhoods; attract 275,000 shoppers; display 700 artists; and top $3 million in sales. The St. James Court Art Show has been named the top fine art and craft show in the country for two consecutive years by Sunshine Artist Magazine, and is named to the Southeast Tourism Society's top 20 event listings.

Historic preservation was the reason the show began so many years ago. Old Louisville, the nation's largest Victorian neighborhood, was officially Louisville's first "subdivision." As a result, the neighborhood must rely on its own funds for the very expensive maintenance needed on a neighborhood with old sewer lines, mature trees, cobblestone sidewalks, intricate landscaping and historic fountains.

Art and craft enthusiasts as well as historical buffs will enjoy walking the streets of this nationally recognized arts destination.

PO Box 3804
Louisville, KY 40201
(502) 635-1842

St. James Court
Art Show

www.stjamescourtartshow.com

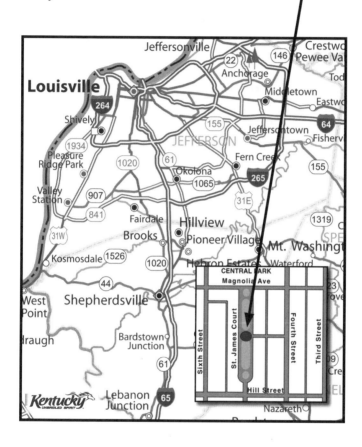

DIRECTIONS: Take I-64E to Louisville; Take I-65S; From I-65 take Exit 135/St. Catherine West; Exiting from either north or south ramps will place you heading west on St. Catherine. Take St. Catherine to 6th Street. Turn left on 6th and continue 4 blocks. Valet parking and on-street parking is available throughout the area

ADMISSION: Free. The event is held rain or shine. No pets, please

HOURS: 2006 Art Show: Oct 6-8; 2007 Art Show: Oct 5-7; Fri-Sat 10-6, Sun 10-5

Oldham County

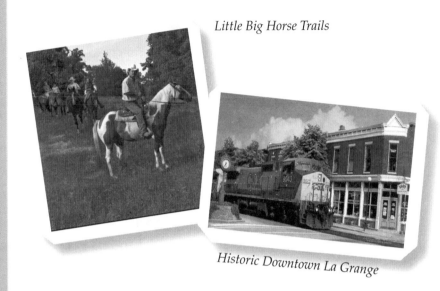

Little Big Horse Trails

Historic Downtown La Grange

On the northeastern fringe of Louisville, a mere 20 minutes from the downtown area, lies the quaint and quiet community of Oldham County. Known for its horse farms, small towns and rolling hills, the county is also emerging as a top choice for visitors looking to experience the intimacy and charm of a small town with proximity to big city amenities.

Things to see

Creasey Mahan Nature Preserve – more than 100 acres with hiking and nature trails, a nature center with Kentucky wildlife displays and a bird observation area; Foxhollow Spa and Manor House Inn– located on a spacious farm, this oasis offers a destination day spa, bed and breakfast, and the greatest variety of massage therapy in the region; Several golf courses: Eagle Creek Golf Course, Oldham County Country Club (semi-private), Nevel Meade, Sleepy Hollow; Little Big Horse Trails – guided horseback riding through scenic trails; Oldham County Community Center – meeting facility with rooms accommodating up to 320 people (kitchen available); Oldham County History Center – Peyton Samuel Head Family Museum, an interactive and interpretive contemporary community museum, housed in a restored historic structure, with a major exhibit on local history and changing exhibits on a variety of topics, including art and natural history; Shops, restaurants, and trains on Main Street. Enjoy unique shopping and dining in historic downtown La Grange, and marvel at the trains that rumble down Main Street. Farmers Market every Saturday June - September. Self-guided walking tours available; Westport Loop – take a trip around KY 524 and visit the Westport General Store, The Tea Kettle, Knock on Wood, the Westport Park, and the county's newest park the Conservation Park, under development; Yew Dell Gardens – a 33-acre home, gardens and arboretum of the late commercial nurseryman Theodore Klein. It is one of 13 American gardens designated as Partnership Gardens by the Garden Conservancy.

The Depot at 412 East Main Street
La Grange, KY 40031
(502) 225-0056 (800) 813-9953
info@oldhamcountytourism.com

Oldham County Tourism

www.oldhamcountytourism.com

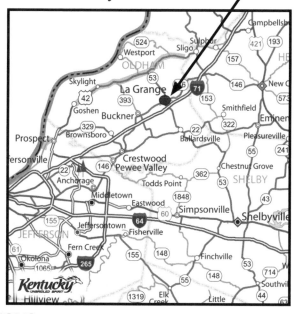

DIRECTIONS: Take I-64E towards Louisville; Take 265N to I-71; Take exit 18 on Hwy; Left on Hwy 393; Turn Right on 146. Just 20 minutes north of downtown Louisville off I-71

ADMISSION: Prices vary, contact Tourism Commission for details

OLDHAM COUNTY - Kentucky Derby Region

Shaker Village of Pleasant Hill

Centre Family Dwelling

The Inn at Shaker Village Guest Room

Shaker Village of Pleasant Hill is the largest restored Shaker community in America, with 34 pristinely restored buildings on 2,900 acres of bluegrass farmland.

Things to see

Shaker Village of Pleasant Hill is pleased to offer guests an assortment of delightful experiences. The Inn at Shaker Village encompasses 81 guest rooms featuring Shaker reproduction furniture, hardwood flooring and private baths. Enjoy breakfast, lunch or dinner in the renowned Trustees' Office Dining Room, featuring traditional Kentucky fare and authentic Shaker specialties. Browse our two village craft stores for handmade items, including Shaker reproduction furniture and many other area crafts.

Interactive village tours wind through this living history site, where interpreters chronicle Shaker life. Within the restored community, artisans work at 19th century trades and historic farming and musical performances bring the past to life. Spend the afternoon exploring the Trails at Shaker Village, which provides hikers, mountain bikers, equestrian riders and carriage drivers an opportunity to explore over 40 miles of trails.

MERCER COUNTY - Bluegrass Region

Modern meeting facilities, nestled among beautiful architecture and rolling countryside, are also offered at Shaker Village of Pleasant Hill. Our professional planners and warm hospitality make Shaker Village an excellent site for your next event. Special events and programs take place throughout the year. Whether it is an antique show, craft fair, music program, workshop or nature program, the village is always full of life.

3501 Lexington Road
Harrodsburg, KY 40330
(859) 734-5411 (800) 734-5611

www.shakervillageky.org

Shaker Village of Pleasant Hill

DIRECTIONS: 24 miles southwest of Lexington, off U.S. 68

ADMISSION: Apr 1-Oct 31: Adults $14; Youth (12-17) $7; Children (6-11) $5; under 6 free. River boat excursion & horse-drawn wagon rides $6 each; Nov 1-Mar 31: Adults $6.50; Youth (12-17) $3.50; Children (6-11) $2.50; under 6 free

HOURS: Apr 1-Oct 31: Mon-Sun 10-5; Nov 1-Mar 31: Mon-Sun 10-4:30; Closed Christmas Eve and Christmas Day

Lawrenceburg-Anderson County

Kentucky River

Tour vineyards and distilleries

Nestled in the heart of the Kentucky Bluegrass region along the Kentucky River, Lawrenceburg is rich in history. From its beginning in the early 1800s, its heritage is preserved today – from Civil War skirmishes, to the grave site of the late great-grandparents of department store founder J.C. Penney. You can learn more about Anna Mac Clarke, the first black woman to enlist during WWII, the evolution of the bourbon industry and the local potential candidate for president. Stories of times past are abundant. Come visit where history is rich, and where bourbon is as old as the community and wines are nationally acclaimed.

Things to see

Four Roses Distillery – visit this continuous-operating distillery, listed on the National Register of Historic Places (www.fourroses.us); Lover's Leap Vineyard and Winery – noted as the largest acreage vineyard in Kentucky, Lover's Leap is a family owned and operated winery (www.loversleapvineyardky.com); Wild Turkey - Austin Nichols Distillery – located above the scenic Kentucky River, this bourbon distillery offers you a peek at how a true American product was born. Take a close-up look at American ingenuity and Kentucky history as this age-old product is made (www.wildturkeybourbon.com); Eagle Lake Flea

Mall – enjoy an afternoon with more than 260 booths of antiques, specialty gifts, hand-made items and lots of miscellaneous collectibles (www.eaglelakefleamall.com).

100 North Main Street, Suite 213
Lawrenceburg KY 40342
(502) 839-5564
info@lawrenceburgky.org

www.lawrenceburgky.org

Anderson County Tourism

Printed in cooperation with the Kentucky Department of Tourism

DIRECTIONS: From Louisville take I-64 East to Exit 48; from Lexington take I-64 West to Exit 53B; from the Bluegrass Pkwy take Exit 59B

ADMISSION: None Charged, tours are free

HOURS: Mon-Fri 8-4

Four Roses Distillery

Visit our distillery and you'll begin to understand why our Bourbon has come to be so mellow. Nestled in the quiet Kentucky countryside near Lawrenceburg, and on the banks of the scenic Salt River, the Four Roses Distillery makes the trip to this very mellow place all that more rewarding. The distillery was built in 1911 and features a unique Spanish Mission-Style architecture rarely seen in Kentucky. It is listed on the National Register of Historic Places and operates continuously except for the summer months, typically July through mid-September. If you are planning a summer trip, be sure to call us at (502) 839-3436 to confirm when we are open.

It began when Paul Jones, Jr., the founder of Four Roses Bourbon, became smitten by the beauty of a Southern belle. It is said that he sent a proposal to her, and she replied that if her answer was "Yes," she would wear a corsage of roses on her gown to the upcoming grand ball. Paul Jones waited for her answer excitedly on that night of the grand ball... when she showed up in her beautiful gown, she wore a corsage of four red roses. He later named his Bourbon "Four Roses" as a symbol of his devout passion for the lovely belle, a passion he thereafter transferred to making his beloved Four Roses Bourbon.

1224 Bonds Mill Rd
Lawrenceburg, KY 40342
Phone: 502-839-3436
info@fourroses.us

www.fourroses.us

Four Roses Distillery

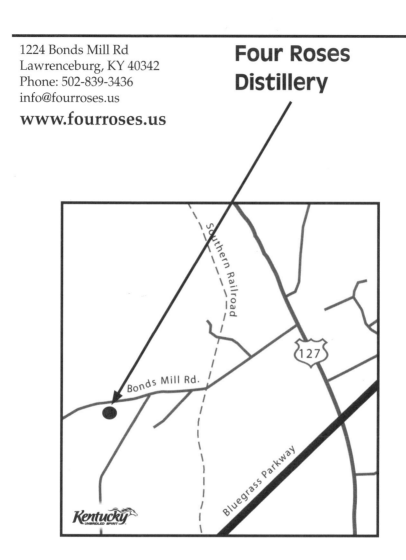

DIRECTIONS: The Distillery is located about 15 miles South of the state's capital, Frankfort. From Lexington, take Bluegrass Parkway to US 127

ADMISSION: Distillery tours are available Mon-Sat, every hour between 9-4. Tours last about 45 minutes and are free of charge. There are no tours on the following dates: Jul 4 and Dec 24-Jan 1

ANDERSON COUNTY - Bluegrass Region

Kentucky Historical Society

Students learn about Kentucky's past in the Old State Capitol

Museum theatre performances bring history to life

The Kentucky Historical Society, a nonprofit organization and an agency of the Kentucky Commerce Cabinet, exists to engage people in the exploration of the commonwealth's diverse heritage. Based at the Thomas D. Clark Center for Kentucky History, KHS encourages its visitors to connect to the past through its museum exhibits, historical tours and research library. The Society's campus includes the Clark Center, the Old State Capitol, and the Kentucky Military History Museum, all located in historic downtown Frankfort.

Things to see

The 167,000-square-foot Thomas D. Clark Center for Kentucky History in downtown Frankfort serves as headquarters for the Kentucky Historical Society. The center is home to two major exhibits, A Kentucky Journey, a 20,000-square-foot permanent exhibit featuring 12,000 years of Kentucky history; the Keeneland Changing Exhibits Gallery, which has featured exhibits on quilts, Kentucky rivers, flags and more; and the Martin F. Schmidt Library, specializing in genealogical research and Kentucky history.

The 1830 Greek Revival Old State Capitol, a National Historic Landmark, served as the capitol of the Commonwealth of Kentucky from 1830 to 1910. Here Kentucky's leaders decided the course their state would take through the tumultuous nineteenth century.

The 1850s Gothic Revival Old State Arsenal, home of the Kentucky Military History Museum, invites visitors to learn more about the service of the Kentucky Militia, State Guard, and other volunteer military organizations, from the Revolution through the Gulf War.

---

100 West Broadway
Frankfort, KY 40601
(502) 564-1792

Kentucky
Historical Society

www.history.ky.gov

DIRECTIONS: From I-64 West, take Exit 53B to U.S. 127, which becomes Clinton St. Turn right onto Ann St, parking is on your left

ADMISSION: (Includes Thomas D. Clark Center for Kentucky History, Old State Capitol and Kentucky Military History Museum) Adults $4; Youths (6-18) $2; Children 5 and under free. KHS members free

HOURS: Exhibits and galleries, Tue-Sat 10-5; Research library, 8-4; closed Sun, Mon and state holidays

FRANKLIN COUNTY - Bluegrass Region

The Woodford Reserve Distillery

Woodford Reserve Visitor's Center

Woodford Reserve barrels

Discover Kentucky's Original Spirit - One Small Batch At A Time

In 1792 Elijah Pepper began making small batches of handcrafted whiskey in a small distillery behind the Woodford County Courthouse in Versailles, Kentucky. As Pepper's business grew, so did his need for a larger distillery and larger source of limestone water. In 1812, on the Grassy Springs branch of Glenn's Creek, located just outside Versailles, Pepper found what he needed.

Today, The Woodford Reserve Distillery, a National Historic Landmark, is known throughout the world as the "Homeplace of Bourbon." Guests who visit the distillery find it much like it was in the 1800s, right down to the copper pot stills. Woodford Reserve is the only distillery in Kentucky using this time-honored and hand-crafted method of production. It is the pot stills that give Woodford Reserve products the unique quality and taste that today's consumer of premium spirits demands and that Elijah Pepper himself would be proud to offer. It is more than just the finest Kentucky bourbon whiskey produced today; It's a rare taste of history.

The 78 acres on which the distillery sits is an idyllic setting amid the rolling countryside of Central Kentucky, which is noted for its beautiful and renowned horse farms. Only at The Woodford Reserve Distillery can one see Kentucky's two most famous products – Bourbon whiskey and thoroughbred horses – maturing side by side.

7855 McCracken Pike
Versailles, KY 40383
(859) 879-1812

The Woodford Reserve Distillery

www.woodfordreserve.com

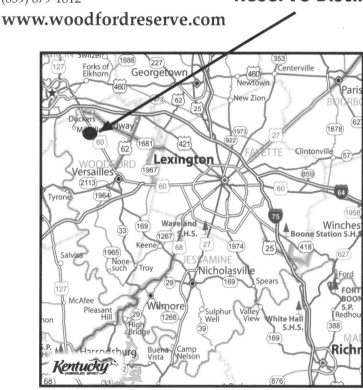

DIRECTIONS: I-64 to U.S. 60 (Frankfort/Versailles Exit 58); turn right toward Versailles; travel for 2.6 miles to Rt. 3360 (Grassy Springs Road); turn right and follow this road until it ends; turn right onto McCracken Pike to Visitors Center

ADMISSION: $5 for guest over 18

HOURS: Nov-Mar: Tue-Sat 9-5, tours at 10, 11, 1, 2 and 3 p.m.; Apr-Oct: Tue-Sat 9-5, Sun 12:30-4:30, tours at 1, 2 and 3 p.m.

WOODFORD COUNTY - Bluegrass Region

Aviation Museum of Kentucky

An aviation paradise for all ages, the Aviation Museum of Kentucky has served as a unique educational and cultural resource of the commonwealth for over 10 years. The Aviation Museum is home to the Kentucky Aviation Hall of Fame, where visitors can learn about notable Kentuckians who made their mark on aviation history. The museum provides a rare opportunity to explore restored aircraft and to recognize the valor and courage of Kentucky's aviators.

Things to see

The Aviation Museum features a changing collection of modern and historic aircraft to delight young and old alike including a U.S. Navy "Blue Angels" A-4 Skyhawk and a rare Crosley Moonbeam biplane. Climb aboard a Kiawa helicopter. Investigate a replica of Kentucky's first aeroplane, the 1908 quadruplane with the world's first retractable landing gear, built and flown in Carter County by aviation pioneer Matthew Sellers.

Aviation Summer Camp is one of the most exciting and popular programs of the Aviation Museum of Kentucky. Girls and boys 10 to 15 years old explore the history, principles and science of flight – then they plan and copilot their own flights in a 4-seat aircraft (with an FAA approved pilot). The camp gives students a taste of the sky as they learn the history of aviation; investigate the principles of flight; examine aircraft and engine design; and find out about careers in aviation.

4316 Hangar Dr
Lexington, KY 40510
(859) 231-1219
www.aviationky.org

The Aviation Museum of Kentucky

DIRECTIONS: Take Versailles Rd (U.S. 60); turn left on Man O' War; turn right on Terminal Dr; turn right onto Air Freight Dr; turn right on Airport Rd; Turn right on Hangar Dr

ADMISSION: Adults (17-59) $5; Seniors (60 and up) $4; Students (6-16) $3; Children (under 6) free; call ahead to schedule groups of 10 or more

HOURS: Tue-Sat 10-5; Sun 1-5; Closed Thanksgiving Day, Christmas Day and New Year's Day

Kentucky's Bluegrass Region

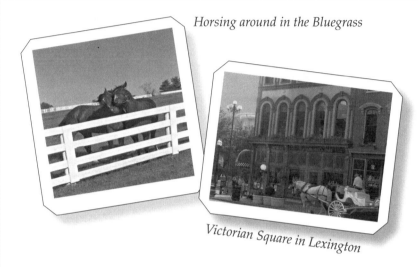

Horsing around in the Bluegrass

Victorian Square in Lexington

Legendary race horses and world renowned Bourbons are the signature products of this unique region. The famed scenic beauty of its rolling hills and lush green pastureland should not be missed. More than 450 manicured horse farms make any drive in the country a memorable experience.

Things to see

Horse farms and training centers, race tracks, historic homes, civil war sites, forts, bourbon distilleries, antique shops, museums, art galleries, folk arts and crafts, outdoor theatre, nature sanctuaries, the Kentucky Horse Park and the world's largest restored Shaker Village can all be explored in central Kentucky's Bluegrass Region. History buffs should not miss Harrodsburg, the first permanent English settlement west of the Allegheny Mountains; Blue Licks State Park, site of the last battle of the Revolutionary War in Kentucky; or the Mary Todd Lincoln House in Lexington, the nation's first shrine to a First Lady.

Lexington, known as the "Horse Capital of the World," is at the heart of the region with dozens of charming small towns around. As the birthplace of bourbon, horse racing legends and great Americans, the Bluegrass Region's unique culture makes it a must-see destination.

Lexington Convention & Visitors Bureau
301 East Vine Street
Lexington, KY 40507
(859) 233-7299 (800) 845-3959
vacation@visitlex.com

Visitor
Information

www.visitlex.com
www.bluegrasskentucky.com

DIRECTIONS: To reach the Visitors Bureau from I-75, take Exit 115 to downtown and follow the Tourist Info signs

HOURS: Year round. Mon-Fri 8:30-5; Sat 10-5; Sun noon-5 in the summer

Keeneland

Equestrian Room

Live Racing – April and October

Keeneland's parklike setting features hundreds of trees that provide spectacular spring blooms and brilliant fall colors. Visitors are welcome to stroll the grounds of this National Historic Landmark year-round. The finest quality Thoroughbred racing is conducted in April and October. Keeneland is also the world's leading Thoroughbred sales company.

Things to see

Discover the Keeneland Gift Shop, considered by many to be the world's finest equine gift shop. You will find the perfect gift for horse lovers of all ages. At Keeneland you can wager on and watch racing from throughout North America year-round. Preferred seating ($3) is available in the Equestrian Room, which features a pub-style menu, more than 100 LCD flat-panel televisions and many tabletop betting terminals.

Whether you attend the races, a special event or simply explore this beautiful attraction, you will experience traditions of pageantry, excitement and hospitality found only at this one-of-a-kind race course in the heart of Kentucky's Bluegrass region.

4201 Versailles Road
Lexington, KY 40510
(859) 254-3412 (800) 456-3412

www.keeneland.com

Keeneland

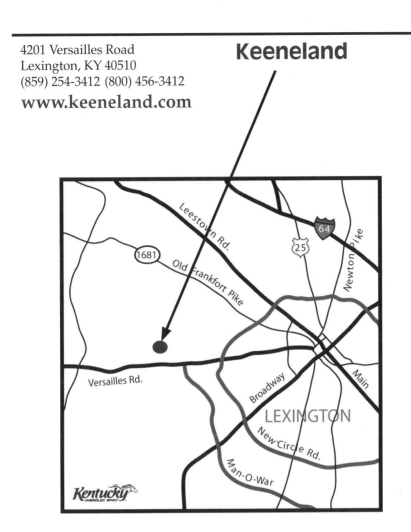

DIRECTIONS: Six miles west of Lexington on Versailles Road (U.S. Hwy 60), adjacent to Blue Grass Airport

ADMISSION: Oct 6-28 Fall race meet; reserved seats $6 weekdays, $8 Sat and Sun (prices include $3 general admission)

HOURS: The Keeneland grounds are open year-round; Racing: Apr and Oct; Simulcasting: year-round (check www.keeneland.com for post times); Keeneland Gift Shop Mon-Sat 9–5

Kentucky Horse Park

Statue of Man o'War

Visitors get up close after the Parade of Breeds

Located in Lexington, the heart of the Bluegrass, the Kentucky Horse Park is a working horse farm with 1,200 acres surrounded by 30 miles of white plank fencing. The park is like none other in the world. Dedicated to man's relationship with the horse, the park features two outstanding museums, twin theaters and 50 different breeds of horses. All of these elements combine to make a visit to the park an enjoyable learning experience for everyone. The park is the place to get close to horses!

Things to see

Man o' War Memorial; Visitor Information Center with the film "Thou Shalt Fly Without Wings"; International Museum of the Horse; American Saddlebred Museum, Kentucky's first native breed; Farrier Shop with a blacksmith exhibiting his iron-pounding craft; the display of different horse breeds in the Breeds Barn. The Draft Horse Barn is an ever-popular stop on the tour.

From March 15 through October 31, the color, sound and excitement of the show ring is captured twice daily in the Parade of Breeds. The excitement of the racetrack and show ring is brought to life by the elite group of champion horses that reside at the park's Hall of Champions.

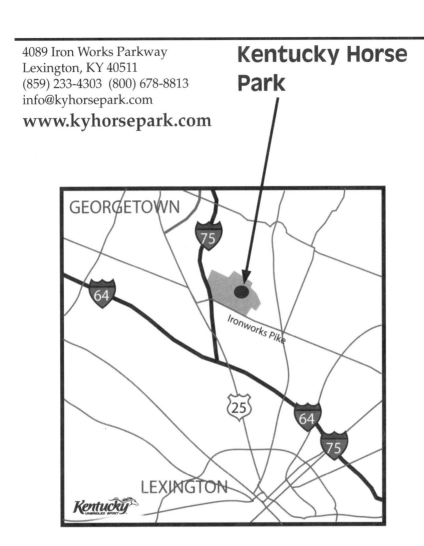

4089 Iron Works Parkway
Lexington, KY 40511
(859) 233-4303 (800) 678-8813
info@kyhorsepark.com
www.kyhorsepark.com

Kentucky Horse Park

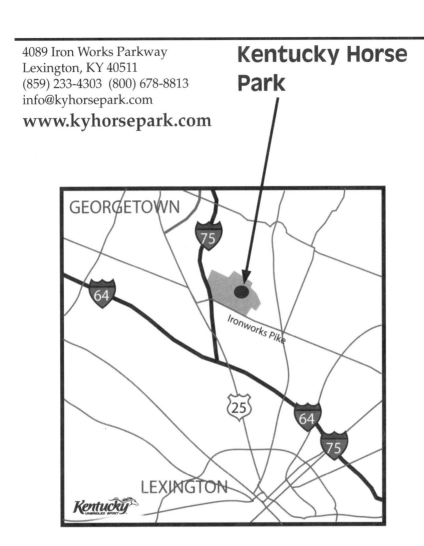

DIRECTIONS: From I-75 take Exit 120 and go east about 1/2 mile.
Park entrance is on the left

ADMISSION: (Includes American Saddlebred Museum)
Nov 1-Mar 14: Adult $9; Child (7-12) $6; Mar 15-Oct 31: Adult $15; Child
(7-12) $8; 6 & under free

HOURS: Nov 1-Mar 14: Open Wed-Sun 9-5; Mar 15-Oct 31: Open 7
days a week 9-5; closed Thanksgiving Eve, Thanksgiving Day, Christmas
Eve, Christmas Day, New Year's Eve and New Year's Day

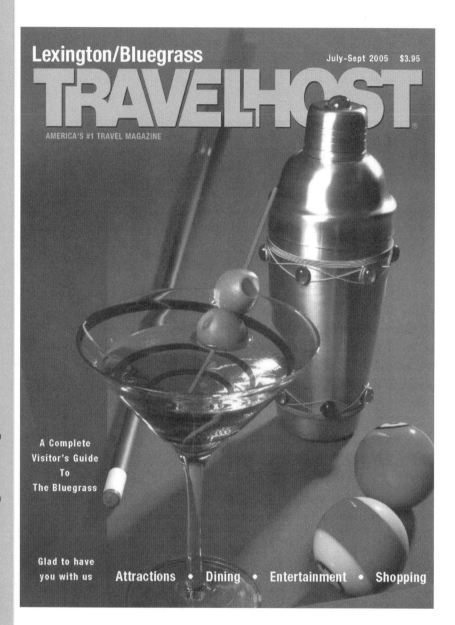

Lexington/Bluegrass

July-Sept 2005 $3.95

TRAVELHOST

AMERICA'S #1 TRAVEL MAGAZINE

A Complete
Visitor's Guide
To
The Bluegrass

Glad to have
you with us   **Attractions • Dining • Entertainment • Shopping**

FAYETTE COUNTY - Bluegrass Region

Kentucky Artisan Center at Berea

Art and craft exhibits

Great shopping for everyone

Located in Berea, the Kentucky Artisan Center showcases the work of Kentucky's many outstanding artisans and cultural heritage attractions found throughout Kentucky.

The Artisan Center features exhibits of Kentucky artisan works, fine art and crafts for sale made by over 700 artisans living all across Kentucky; Kentucky travel assistance; and a café that specializes in Kentucky cuisine.

Artisan works for sale at the center include pottery, glass, jewelry and other crafts; paintings; music; books; and specialty food items—works both traditional and innovative in style–all made in Kentucky. There is something for every price range—recordings by Kentucky musicians; books by Kentucky authors and publishers; and specialty food products by Kentucky agricultural producers. Artisan demonstrations are also held on Fridays and Saturdays at the center.

In the center's dining area, visitors will find everything from snacks to sandwiches and full dinners featuring Kentucky specialties. Some of the entrees include meatloaf, Southern fried chicken, rotisserie chicken and fried catfish. Homemade desserts and the Café's signature dessert, piping hot Bread Pudding with Bourbon sauce, are also available.

In the front lobby, staff can help you plan further travels in Kentucky. And only two miles away in downtown Berea, the Folk Art and Crafts Capital of Kentucky, visitors can visit great art and craft galleries and tour working artisan studios. You'll want to make visiting the Kentucky Artisan Center in Berea a regular part of your travel plans.

975 Walnut Meadow Road
Berea, KY 40403
(859) 985-5448

Kentucky Artisan Center at Berea

**www.kentuckyartisan
center.ky.gov**

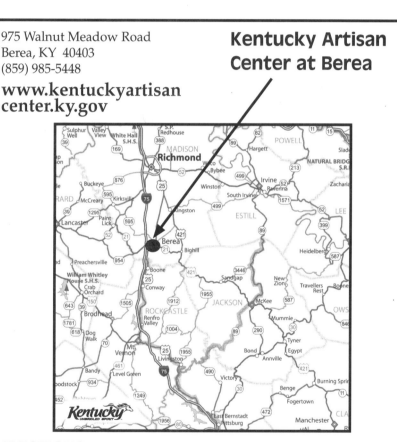

DIRECTIONS: Located off I-75 at Exit 77, 40 miles south of Lexington

ADMISSION: No charge

HOURS: Daily 8-8; closed Christmas Day, New Year's Day and Thanksgiving Day

Winchester-Clark County

Bluegrass Heritage Museum

Civil War Fort at Boonesboro

Centrally located, Winchester and Clark County offer breathtaking scenery, great history nestled in rich traditions and a friendly smile. We welcome you to come visit the past, but don't be surprised to discover that Winchester and Clark County not only have great history but a bright future.

Things to see

Take a guided walking tour of downtown on Thursday and Friday throughout the summer or by appointment. Downtown Winchester, listed on the National Register of Historic Places, is filled with quaint shops and wonderful restaurants. **Leeds Center for the Arts**, located on North Main Street, the Art Deco theater offers cultural and community events including plays, musicals, concerts, classes, seminars and children's programming. Visit www.leedscenter.com. **Lower Howard's Creek Nature and Heritage Preserve** was established as a Kentucky State Nature Preserve on nearly 300 acres of land. Come hike alongside spectacular waterfalls and historical 18th century structures on guided tours only. Visit www.lowerhowardscreek.org. **The Civil War Fort at**

Boonesboro is located on Ford Road overlooking the Kentucky River. The earthen works fortification was manned by African American soldiers as part of the defense system of the Kentucky River. Self-guided tours year round, guided tours by appointment. **The Bluegrass Heritage Museum**, located on South Main Street, provides visitors with insight to the rich history of Winchester, Clark County and the Region. The museum is open Tuesday through Saturday 12-6 (www.bgheritage. com)

---

2 South Maple Street
Winchester, KY 40391
(859) 744-0556   (800) 298-9105
info@tourwinchester.com

Winchester-Clark County Tourism

www.tourwinchester.com

DIRECTIONS: I-64 to Exit 96; turn right and travel through 2 lights; office at third light

ADMISSION: Prices vary, contact Tourism Office for details

HOURS: Mon-Fri 8-5; closed 12-1

Carrollton-Carroll County

General Butler State Resort Park Golf Course

Butler-Turpin State Historic House

Carrollton is an area steeped in history. From General Butler State Resort Park, which encompasses 790 acres, to Carrollton's Point Park where you can view the converging of the mighty Ohio and Kentucky rivers, there is never a lack of options. Spend a lazy day watching river traffic float by, or drive through the historic town where you can find the Masterson House, the oldest two-story brick home still standing on the Ohio between Pittsburgh and Cairo, Illinois. Venture onto the state park grounds and tour the Butler-Turpin State Historic House and Butler Family cemetery. With activities at the state park such as paddleboat rentals, miniature golf, swimming, fishing and a regulation 9-hole golf course there are plenty of things to do. Carrollton is a place where you still hear the church bells at noon, see parades down the main thoroughfare, and where you are always greeted by a smile. With their small town charm, you almost forget how close you are to Louisville and Cincinnati. With just 50 miles separating you from either city, Carrollton is the ideal place to stay, so you can be in the middle of it all.

515 Highland Avenue
PO Box 293
Carrollton, KY 41008
(800) 325-4290 (502) 732-7036
info@carrolltontourism.com

Carrollton-Carroll County Tourism

www.carrolltontourism.com

DIRECTIONS: Take I-75 N to I-71 S; take Exit 44, turn right, go four miles into Downtown Business District, Visitors Center is on your right

ADMISSION: Some tours are free, others available for a small fee. Contact the Visitors Center for more information.

HOURS: Mon-Fri 9-5; Sat 9-2; closed on Sun

Newport Aquarium

Sweet Pea

Denver

If you're looking for an exciting, entertaining and educational place to visit, plan on an awe-inspiring trip to the Newport Aquarium in Northern Kentucky. Recently named the top aquarium in the Midwest by the prestigious Zagat survey, the Newport Aquarium is a water wonderland your family will love. You'll be thrilled by thousands of exotic fish and animals in this magical underwater world that includes over 55 sharks and one of the only shark rays on display in the world. We call her "Sweet Pea." You'll call her one of the most captivating creatures you've ever seen.

Beginning in the summer of 2006, you can enjoy the most unique experience of its kind in the region – our new Shark Central Exhibit. It's home to a field research facility and dozens of sharks you can actually touch. You'll learn the official "two-finger touch" technique and how to properly pet sharks. It's safe. It's thrilling. It's an experience your kids will never forget.

You'll not only enjoy a wide-range of exhibits, animals and aquatic life from sharks to penguins to free-flying lorikeets you can feed by hand, you can take part in family-friendly events throughout the year during Halloween, Christmas, Valentine's Day and even Derby Day.

Newport on the Levee
One Aquarium Way
Newport, KY 41071
(859) 261-7444 (800) 406-3474
info@newportaquarium.com

Newport Aquarium

www.newportaquarium.com

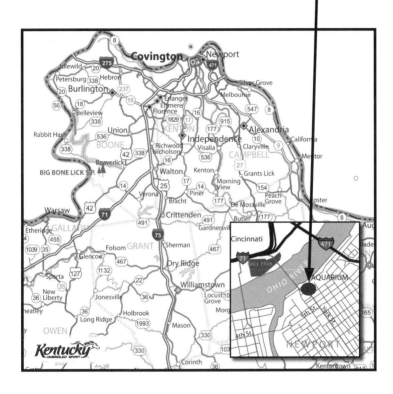

DIRECTIONS: Take I-75 N to Covington 5th St Exit; follow signs to Aquarium; Easily accessible from I-275, I-471, I-75 and I-71. Visit www. newportaquarium.com for details

ADMISSION: Adults $17.95; Seniors (65+) $15.95; Kids (3-12) $10.95; Children 2 and under are admitted free

HOURS: Open 365 days a year: 10-6, with extended hours Memorial Day through Labor Day. Visit www.newportaquarium.com for summer and holiday hours.

Maysville-Mason County

Nestled along the Ohio River in Northern Kentucky, Maysville is just 1½ hours from I-75 in Lexington, Kentucky and Cincinnati, Ohio. Scenic river views, pioneer and underground railroad history, outdoor recreation, relaxation and small town charm are just a few of the amenities we offer visitors. Stay for a day or the weekend and discover why "We're More Than Just History."

Things to see

History & Heritage: Daily tours of Washington Historic District are available from the Washington Visitors Center, 11 a.m. to 3 p.m. Costumed tour guides lead you through this authentic 1780s pioneer village; guided walking & trolley tours of downtown Maysville Historic District available by appointment; National Underground Railroad Museum; Museum Center & Research Library; African American heritage sites; floodwall murals and a variety of 1800s architectural styles found in downtown Maysville; Self-Guided Tour of Maysville's Historic Districts Brochure available from Maysville-Mason County Tourism Office and Washington Visitors Center; **Recreation:** swimming, fishing, tennis, picnicking at Maysville-Mason County Recreation Park; Paradise Breeze Water Park; two public 18-hole golf courses; farm tours; ATV & dirt bike park; pay lake fishing; Maysville River Park & Marina; camping; scenic country roads for bicycling; horseback riding and Limestone Landing Fishing Pier.

216 Bridge Street
Maysville, KY 41056
(606) 564-9419

www.cityofmaysville.com

Maysville-Mason County Tourism

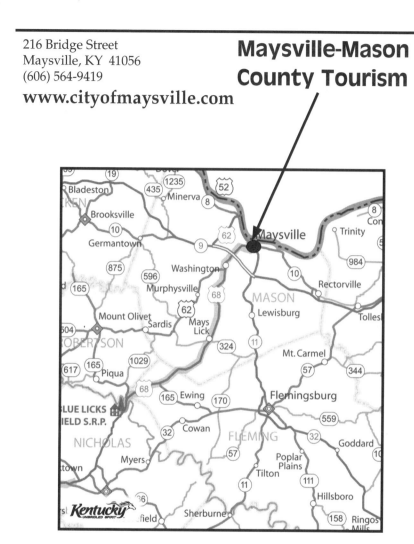

DIRECTIONS: From Lexington take I-75 to Exit 113, travel north on U.S. Hwy 68 approximately 65 miles. Northern Kentucky/Cincinnati, Ohio take KY 9 (AA Hwy) east, approximately 55 miles

ADMISSION: Prices vary, contact Tourism Office for details

Mount Sterling-Montgomery County

Scenic drive

Historic Downtown Mt. Sterling

Whether you visit Mount Sterling for a day, a weekend or a week, you'll feel right at home while being nestled in the foothills of the Appalachian Mountains and the Kentucky Bluegrass Region. During your stay at one of the *100 Best Communities for Young People*, become one of the many visitors who have fallen in love with our charming historical downtown that is unique with an art gallery, gift shops and restaurants.

Things to see

Play a round of golf at Old Silo, one of Kentucky's best public golf courses; take an individual or a group personalized tour of Bramble Ridge Apple Orchard, home of Kentucky's largest apple slingshot; tour the Ruth Hunt Candy Factory, home of the official candy of Churchill Downs and the Kentucky Derby®; during the month of October, visit Two Sister's Pumpkin Patch where a hayride takes you to pick your one-of-a-kind pumpkin; visit Heavenly View Farm Bed and Breakfast; and then take a scenic drive to see the first quilt block of the Gateway Quilt Trail located on the barn of Sterling Thimble Quilt Shop.

Last but certainly not least be sure to visit us for our biggest event of the year, October Court Day, one of Kentucky's oldest traditional festivals in downtown Mount Sterling. It truly is something you have to do at least once in your life!

126 West Main Street
Mount Sterling, KY 40353
(859) 498-8732   (866) 415-7439
mtourism@mis.net
www.mtsterlingtourism.com

Mount Sterling-Montgomery County Tourism

DIRECTIONS: Mount Sterling is located 25 minutes east of Lexington. Take I-64 to Exit 110

ADMISSION: Prices vary, call the Tourism Office for details

HOURS: Mon-Fri 8-4:30

MONTGOMERY COUNTY - Eastern Highlands North Region

Ruth Hunt Candy Company

Factory and store

Hand-stirred caramels

It all began in the kitchen of her Mt. Sterling home, where Ruth Tharpe Hunt served homemade sweets to her bridge club. In 1921 she decided to start a small candy business. Today, still located in Mt. Sterling, Ruth Hunt Candies remains a Kentucky landmark. From cinnamon suckers being formed on huge old marble slabs, to caramels stirred in spun copper kettles, our factory is flavored with sights and smells of good old-fashioned, homemade candy. Throughout the years a strict adherence to quality has been observed. Candy makers use only the finest of ingredients, and no waxes are added to our chocolate! Ruth Hunt Candies is proud to be distinguished as "The Official Candymakers of Churchill Downs® and The Kentucky Derby®."

Ruth Hunt produces over 100 varieties of candies, including traditional pulled cream candy, Woodford Reserve Bourbon Balls, Blue Monday Candy Bars and Jamieson's Chocolate, a full line of dark chocolate bars imported from Ghana, West Africa. Many of our products are packed in boxes featuring a Thoroughbred racing scene beneath the historic twin spires of Churchill Downs. In addition to our confectionary specialties, our store features many equine-related items and a variety of Kentucky-made crafts and food products.

550 North Maysville Rd
Mount Sterling, KY 40353
(800) 927-0302
info@ruthhuntcandy.com
www.ruthhuntcandy.com

Ruth Hunt Candy Company

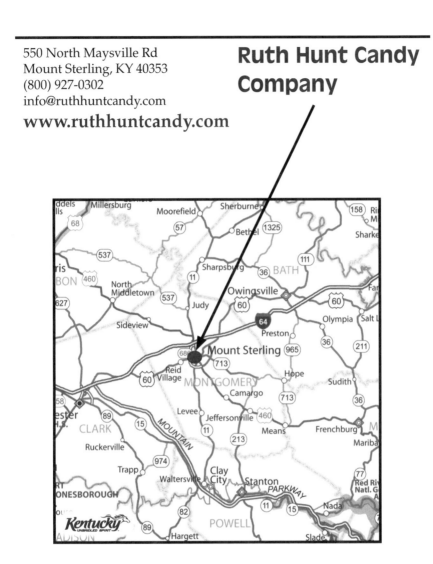

DIRECTIONS: From I-64 take Exit 110; go south toward downtown on Hwy 460/11. We are 1/3 of a mile from the exit, on the right

ADMISSION: Free factory tours; call ahead for groups and to inquire about work schedules

HOURS: The store is open Mon-Sat 9-5:30; Sun 1-5:30; closed Thanksgiving, Christmas Day & Easter Sunday

MONTGOMERY COUNTY - Eastern Highlands North Region

More than Music

Ricky Skaggs

A Heritage Driving Tour of Route 23

"Hi, I'm Ricky Skaggs and I'd like to invite you on a journey with me down Route 23 in Eastern Kentucky, my home territory." Those are the opening words of this audio driving tour and companion book that guide you along the cultural landscape of Route 23 with stories from musicians that have gone on to reach national fame and local people who are proud to share their heritage.

As you wind down the Country Music Highway, Ricky will point out the places of interest; the people that live and work in the areas you visit will fill in the details. The tour even invites you to family reunions and tells you who welcomes tourists to stop by for a glass of lemonade and a local history lesson on their front porch.

The package includes the book with maps, history and photos along with telephone numbers, web sites and a calendar of events. There are three CDs to guide you from crossing the Ohio River into Kentucky, down to Jenkins near the Virginia border, along with side trips to smaller communities like Butcher Holler, David and Sandy Hook. A fourth bonus CD is a sampler of music by artists with ties to the region including

Dwight Yoakum, Ricky Skaggs, Loretta Lynn, Crystal Gayle, the Stanley Brothers and The Judds.

More than Music

This audio driving tour was produced by the Kentucky Folklife Program, an interagency program of the Kentucky Arts Council (www.artscouncil. ky.gov) and the Kentucky Historical Society (www.history.ky.gov); both state agencies in the Commerce Cabinet. Funding was made possible through a transportation enhancement grant funded by the Kentucky Department of Transportation and the Kentucky Arts Council, with support from the National Endowment for the Arts.

PRICE: $24.99

WHERE TO PURCHASE:

"More than Music" can be purchased online through the Kentucky Historical Society's 1792 store at **http://store. kentucky.gov/kyhs** or at the following locations:

- Ashland Convention and Visitors Bureau, Route 23, Ashland; (606) 329-1007, www.visitashlandky.com
- The Paveillon, Route 23, Louisa; (606) 638-9998
- Country Music Highway Museum, 120 Starves Branch Road, Paintsville; (606) 297-1469
- The Mountain Arts Center, Route 23, Prestonsburg; (606) 889-9125, www. macarts.com
- David Appalachian Crafts, Hwy. 404, David; (606) 886-2377, www. davidappalachiancrafts.com
- Cozy Corner Gifts and Bookstore, Main Street, Whitesburg; (606) 633-9637

Wurtland-Greenup County

Greenbo Lake State Resort Park

McConnell House quilt project

Nestled between the foot hills of Appalachia and the scenic Ohio River lies Greenup County. Established in 1803 and named for a former governor, Greenup County offers every visitor a unique experience Whether it be a relaxing getaway in the Jesse Stuart Lodge at Greenbo Lake State Resort Park or an adventurous back road trek to experience our covered bridges, any visit will be a memorable one.

History buffs will want to be sure and visit the McConnell House, the Court House in downtown Greenup or the Bryson General Store for a trip back in time. Completed in 1955 the Greenup Lock & Dam is a marvel of concrete that holds the mighty Ohio within its banks both up and down the river in Greenup County and offers one of the greatest sauger fisheries in the fall of the year. A visit to the observation deck of the lock is a must for any traveler. Are you hungry yet? Sample the fair of many area restaurants including the State Park Lodge Dining Area, Gurbers and Amire's Pizza of Flatwoods. Speaking of Flatwoods, look close you just may get a glimpse of native son Billy Ray Cyrus. Cyrus, who graduated form Russell High School got his start here and still returns to the area every chance his "Achy Breaky Heart" will allow.

Come to Greenup for the beauty and stay for the relaxation. Hope to see ya soon.

---

100 McConnell House Drive
Wurtland, KY 41144
(606) 834-0007   (877) 868-7473
Info@TourGreenupCounty.com
www.TourGreenupCounty.com

Greenup County Tourism Commission

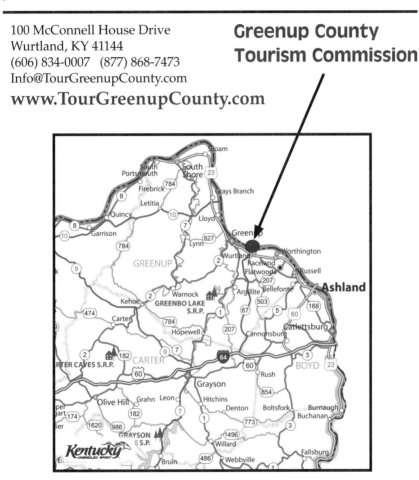

DIRECTIONS: From I-64 take the Industrial Pkwy exit into Greenup; at U.S. 23, go straight through the light and the McConnell House, where the Tourism Commission is located, will be on the left

ADMISSION: No cost for admission

HOURS: Tours of the McConnell House are conducted Mon-Fri from 9-3

Ashland Area

Paramount Theater

The Judd's

Throughout the year, Ashland offers a pleasing blend of history, culture, scenic venues, outdoor recreation and annual festivals, guaranteed to provide you with true Southern Hospitality! Ashland, Boyd and Greenup counties are situated on the Ohio River where the Bluegrass State meets neighboring Ohio and West Virginia. Today, Ashland, Huntington, W. Va. and Ironton, Ohio form a vibrant metropolitan tri-state area of more than 300,000 people, making this area not only culturally alive, but culturally diverse. Located in the heart of the U.S., Ashland is minutes from I-64 and a direct link on the colorful U.S. 23 – Country Music Highway. This accessibility makes Ashland a perfect stop for your travels.

Things to see

Recreational and cultural opportunities abound, with nearby state parks and man-made lakes. Downtown Ashland's 33-acre Central Park offers ball fields, tennis courts, play grounds and mature trees. A publicly owned Tennis Center with 12 outdoor and four indoor courts, and first-class high school athletic facilities add to the recreational mix. Downtown Ashland features the Highlands Museum and Discovery Center, the new Pendleton Artist Center, the Paramount Performing Arts

Center (recently restored and enlarged), the Ashland Art Gallery and the Jesse Stuart Foundation.

Annual celebrations include Poage Landing Days in September, Summer Motion in July, the Catlettsburg Memorial Day Parade, and Central Park's Winter Wonderland of Lights at Christmas.

1509 Winchester Avenue
Ashland, KY 41101
(606) 329-1007 (800) 377-6249
aacvb@visitashlandky.com
www.visitashlandky.com

Ashland Area Convention & Visitors Bureau

DIRECTIONS: Take I-64 E to Exit 1841; turn right on Winchester Ave

ADMISSION: Prices vary, contact the Visitors Bureau for details

HOURS: Mon-Fri 9-5

Jesse Stuart Foundation

The place to find books about Kentucky and Appalachia

JSF Bookstore

Located in Ashland, the Jesse Stuart Foundation is the place to find books about Kentucky and Appalachia. The gift shop offers a variety of Kentucky arts and crafts. The Leming Gallery features traveling exhibits, as well as permanent works. Bargain hunters will find great selection in the used book store. Collectors can purchase Jesse Stuart signed books, First Editions and other collectible items.

We at the Jesse Stuart Foundation are deeply committed to our dual mission of preserving the human and literary legacy of Jesse Stuart while fostering appreciation of the Appalachian way of life through our book publishing and other activities. The JSF has reprinted many of Stuart's out-of-print books along with other books that focus on Kentucky and Appalachia. The JSF promotes a number of cultural and educational programs and encourages the study of Jesse Stuart's works and related regional materials. Our primary purpose is to produce books which supplement the educational system at all levels. We have thousands of books in stock and we want to make them accessible to teachers and librarians, as well as general readers. We also promote Stuart's legacy through videotapes, dramas, readings and other presentations for school and civic groups, and an annual Jesse Stuart Weekend at Greenbo Lake State Resort Park. We are proud of the fact that we have become a significant regional press and bookseller and a major source of books for readers of all ages.

1645 Winchester Avenue
Ashland, KY 41101
(606) 326-1667 (800) 504-0209
www.JSFBOOKS.com

Jesse Stuart
Foundation

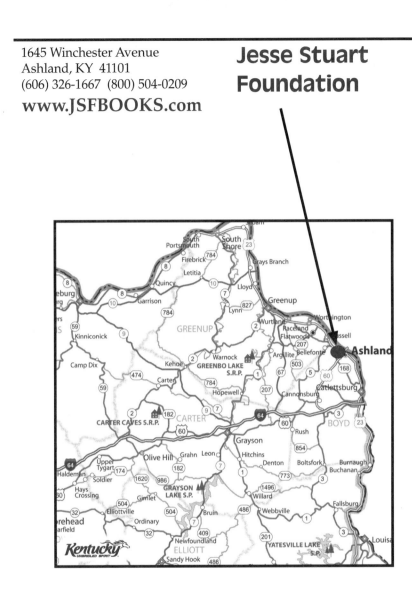

DIRECTIONS: I-64 west to Exit 191; turn north on U.S. 23 and go approximately 8 miles; U.S. 23 becomes Winchester Ave. in Ashland. The JSF is located at the corner of Winchester and 17th Streets

ADMISSION: Free

HOURS: Mon-Fri 9-5; closed Sat and Sun

Paintsville-Johnson County

Loretta Lynn's Birthplace

Country Music Highway Museum

Paintsville, the county seat of Johnson County, is located in the heart of the Appalachian Mountains. The history of Paintsville dates back to 1790 when a Virginia colonel named John Preston came with a group of trappers and traders to establish a trading post for furs and hardware. Today, Paintsville is known for its progressive growth and tourism attractions. Johnson County is proud to be home to such entertainers as Loretta Lynn, Crystal Gayle, Hylo Brown and Richard Thomas. The Paintsville Tourism and Information Center offers custom tour itineraries, reunion and special event planning and a travel planner's itinerary guide. Also, Paintsville is the site of the world's longest plastic pedestrian bridge.

Things to see

Birthplace of Country Music Legend Loretta Lynn at Butcher Holler in Van Lear; Country Music Highway Museum; 1850s Mountain Homeplace where costumed interpreters share life in Appalachia during this time period; Van Lear Historical Museum (Coal Miners' Museum);

Paintsville Golf Course; and Paintsville Lake State Park & Campground.

Major events include the Red Bud Gospel Sing (Memorial Day Weekend), Craft Fair (July), Van Lear Days (August), Kentucky Apple Festival (October), and Ol' Fashion Christmas at Mountain Homeplace. Fall events include: Haunted Trail, Haunted Museums, Storytelling (October), Holiday Happenings Craft Fair (November).

---

100 Staves Branch Road
Paintsville, KY 41240
(800) 542-5790   (606) 297-1469
tourpvill@foothills.net

Paintsville Tourism

www.paintsville.org/tourism

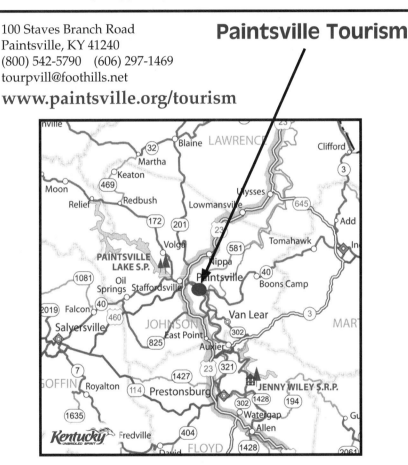

DIRECTIONS: I-64 E to Mountain Pkwy; turn left on U.S. 460; take KY 23 to Paintsville/Stafforsville Exit

ADMISSION: Prices vary, contact Tourism Center for details

HOURS: Mon-Fri 8-4

JOHNSON COUNTY - Eastern Highlands South Region

Jenny Wiley Theatre

The Legend of Jenny Wiley

Disney's Beauty and The Beast

Jenny Wiley Theatre is Kentucky's only professional theatre east of I-75, offering theatrical productions all year long at both the Jenny Wiley Amphitheatre, located within the Jenny Wiley State Resort Park, and the nearby Mountain Arts Center in Prestonsburg. The Theatre's presentations of classic Broadway musicals, comedies, historical dramas and holiday productions have kept theatre-goers entertained for over 40 years. Come enjoy the best entertainment the region has to offer and make Jenny Wiley Theatre a tradition in your family for years to come!

Things to see

Jenny Wiley Theatre offers professional theatre in rotating repetition so audiences can see as many as four shows in one weekend.

2006 Season productions include: *The Music Man*, *The Legend of Jenny Wiley*, *Nunsense* and *Footloose*.

2006 Fall Production (at the Mountain Arts Center): *The Legend of Sleepy Hollow*, Holiday Production: *It's A Wonderful Life* (location to be determined).

FLOYD COUNTY - Eastern Highlands North Region

121 Theatre Court
Prestonsburg, KY 41653
(606) 886-9274 (877) CALL-JWT
tickets@jwtheatre.com

www.jwtheatre.com

Jenny Wiley
Theatre

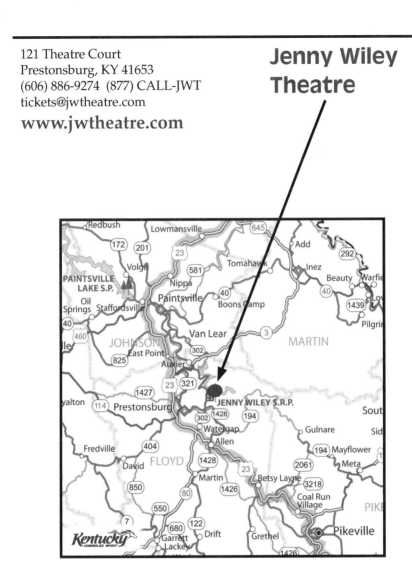

DIRECTIONS: I-64 E to Mountain Pkwy; turn right on Hwy 114; from U.S. 23 take the Martin/Hazard Exit (Route 80/302) 3 miles to Jenny Wiley Theatre

ADMISSION: Adult $21, Seniors $19, Youth $13, Meal Shows $35

HOURS: Box Office Tue-Sat 10am-9pm; Sun 1pm-9pm; Mon 10am-6pm

Mountain Arts Center

The Kentucky Opry at the Mountain Arts Center

(l-r) Freddie Goble and Keith Caudill

In October 1996 the Mountain Arts Center hosted its grand opening and the cultural fabric of Eastern Kentucky has not been the same since. This beautiful facility, located within a stone's throw of U.S. 23 "Country Music Highway," houses a 1,050 seat (very intimate) theater – where the last row in the theater is only 26 rows from the stage, several large meeting rooms, a commercial recording/video editing studio, and art gallery.

The Mountain Arts Center is located near Prestonsburg on U.S. 23 "Country Music Highway," which is certainly appropriate. Our state-of-the-art venue plays host to national headlining acts from a wide range of musical backgrounds – bluegrass, gospel, rock and of course, country music – including many of Eastern Kentucky's favorite sons and daughters. During its tenure, the MAC has hosted performances by major country and bluegrass stars (Dwight Yoakam, Loretta Lynn, George Jones, Montgomery Gentry, Ricky Skaggs, Patty Loveless, Ralph Stanley, IIIrd Tyme Out, Merle Haggard), rock and roll groups (The Temptations, Percy Sledge, The Platters, The Drifters), gospel greats (The Kingsmen, The Bishops, John Hagee, Dottie Rambo, Steve Green), family theater (Always Patsy Cline, Annie, The King and I, Nutcracker, On Golden Pond), big bands (the Tommy Dorsey and Glenn Miller Orchestras), and many other nationally acclaimed artists...the list seems endless!

With its state-of-the-art theater, large meeting rooms, expansive lobby and professional staff, the Mountain Arts Center is more than an entertainment venue.

The Mountain Arts Center is the home of the Kentucky Opry. The Opry's singers and musicians blend country, bluegrass, gospel and pop music with dazzling lights, costumes and mountain humor which will entertain the entire family.

50 Hal Rogers Drive
Prestonsburg, KY 41653
606-889-9125
info@macarts.com

www.macarts.com

Mountain Arts Center

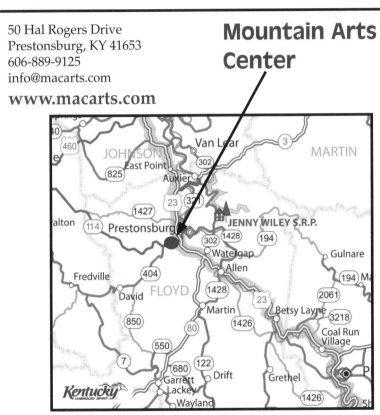

DIRECTIONS: Follow the Mountain Parkway to Campton, stay left and follow the signs to Prestonsburg/Salyersville, just before Prestonsburg, the Mountain Arts Center will be on your left; from Ashland, go south on U.S. 23

ADMISSION: Kentucky Opry ticket prices: Adults $15; Seniors (55+) $13; Students (under 18) $11. Group rates available – call for rate. Tickets on other performances vary, call (888) 622-2787

Pikeville-Pike County

Breaks Interstate Park

Whitewater rafting, Russell Fork River

Located in the beautiful mountains of Eastern Kentucky, Pikeville is the location of the famous cut-through project, an engineering marvel, and the largest earth moving project since the Panama Canal. Pike County is also the site of the infamous feud between the Hatfields and McCoys. We celebrate our heritage in the spring with Hillbilly Days Festival in downtown Pikeville and Apple Blossom Festival in Elkhorn City.

Things to see

Breaks Interstate Park, which has the largest canyon east of the Mississippi River, offers an array of outdoor activities and breathtaking scenery; Fishtrap Lake State Park – a beautiful lake nestled between mountains with picnic areas and marina, and Pine Mountain Trail State Park (a unique linear park that runs along the top of the Pine Mountain); Mountain Pub Links Golf Course; Hatfield & McCoy Feud audio driving tour (a guide to sites where the feud took place); Heritage museums, historic Dils Cemetery, where members of the McCoy Family are buried and Artists Collaborative Theatre which presents a variety of performances each year.

From November 15-December 31, experience Mountain Top Lights, a spectacular drive-through light show, beautifully displayed within the

Breaks Interstate Park with animated scenes reflecting the originality of Eastern Kentucky.

781 Hambley Blvd.
Pikeville, KY 41501
(606) 432-5063 (800) 844-7453
tourpikeco@setel.com
www.tourpikecounty.com

Pikeville-Pike County Tourism

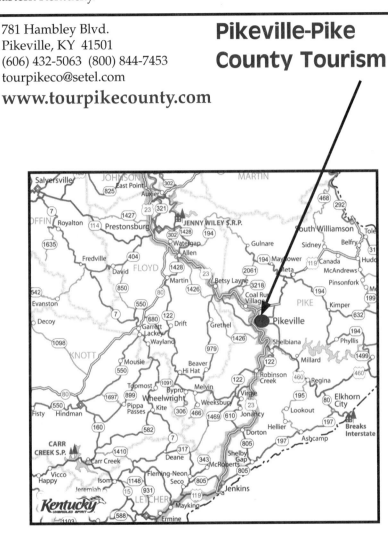

DIRECTIONS: Take I-64 E to Mountain Pkwy (becomes Hwy 114); merge onto U.S. 23 N

ADMISSION: Prices vary, contact Tourism Office for details

HOURS: Hours of operation vary, contact Tourism Office for details

PIKE COUNTY - Eastern Highlands North Region

Cumberland Gap National Historical Park

Poets, songwriters, novelists, journal writers, historians and artists have captured the grandeur of the Cumberland Gap. James Smith, in his journal of 1792, penned what is perhaps one of the most poignant descriptions of this national and historically significant landmark: "We started just as the sun began to gild the tops of the high mountains. We ascended Cumberland Mountain, from the top of which the bright luminary of day appeared to our view in all his rising glory; the mists dispersed and the floating clouds hasted away at his appearing. This is the famous Cumberland Gap..." Thanks to the vision of Congress, who in 1940 authorized Cumberland Gap National Historical Park, visitors today can still bask in its beauty and immerse themselves in its rich history.

The story of the first doorway to the west is commemorated at Cumberland Gap National Historical Park, located in southeast Kentucky, southwest Virginia, and northeast Tennessee where the borders of the three states meet. Carved by wind and water, Cumberland Gap forms a major break in the formidable Appalachian Mountain chain. First used by large game animals in their migratory journeys and followed by American Indians, the Cumberland Gap was the first and best avenue for settlement of the interior of this nation. From 1775 to 1810, the Gap's heyday, between 200,000 and 300,000 men, women, and children crossed the Gap into the new frontier, the unknown land of "Kentuckee."

Cumberland Gap National Historical Park is a wonderful tapestry of historical, cultural, and natural resources woven intricately together. In July and in October the mountains come alive with brilliant fall foliage.

US 25E South
PO Box 1848
Middlesboro, KY 40965
(606) 248-2817
www.nps.gov/cuga

Cumberland Gap National Historical Park

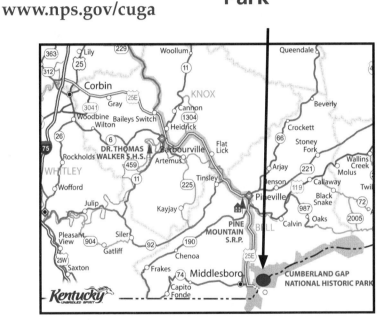

DIRECTIONS: I-75 S to Corbin; take 25E to Middlesboro

ADMISSION: No entrance fee; donation box is located in the Visitor Center; camping: $10/night for sites without electricity; $15/night for sites with electricity; nominal fee and reservations required for some ranger-guided activities

HOURS: Visitor Center: Memorial Day-Labor Day, daily 8-6; Labor Day-Memorial Day, daily 8-5; closed Christmas Day and New Year's Day; Park Grounds are open daily

BELL COUNTY - Eastern Highlands South Region

Barbourville-Knox County

Following the Revolutionary War, Barbourville's location on the Wilderness Road from Cumberland Gap earned it the right to be part of "the First Frontier."

In the Barbourville Municipal building, the Knox Historical Museum has one of the largest displays of items representing Kentucky mountain history in the southeastern corner of the state. Ranging from prehistoric and Native American artifacts arranged by archaeological periods to a modern moonshine still captured only a few years ago, the museum has numerous frontier period items, an early medical exhibit, and a turn-of-the-century country store display.

Barbourville is wealthy in recreational parks, but the crown jewel of the set is the Barbourville Recreational Park, which showcases the Brickyard Waves Waterpark, with its twisting and long water slide, wave pool, and lazy river.

Five miles from Barbourville is the Dr. Thomas Walker State Park Historical Site, a recreational park with a replica of the cabin built by the Walker party during their exploration in the spring of 1750.

Only a couple of miles north of Barbourville is the Kentucky

Communities Craft Village. Along a gently rising hillside, three authentic log cabins filled with traditional mountain crafts give those interested in local crafts the feeling that they are buying directly from a mountain homestead.

196 Daniel Boone Drive, Suite 205
Barbourville, KY 40906
(606) 546-4300

Barbourville Tourism Commission

www.knoxcochamber.com

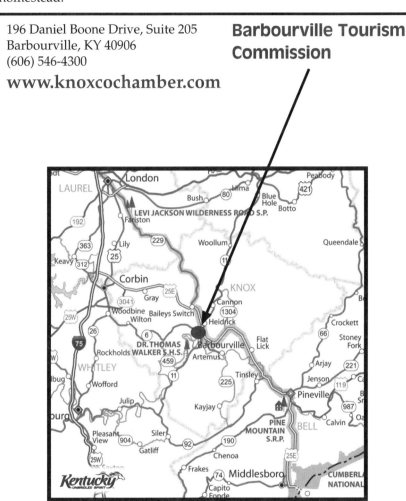

DIRECTIONS: I-75 S to Corbin; take 25 E to Barbourville

ADMISSION: Prices vary, call Tourism Commission for details

Williamsburg

Cumberland Falls

Kentucky Splash Water Park

At first glance, Williamsburg might look like any other sleepy town in southeastern Kentucky. But a better look will tell you that it's anything but sleepy. Nestled between the Cumberland River, the Daniel Boone National Forest and the Appalachian Mountains is a community changed by time but rich in cultural heritage.

Things to see

Williamsburg features some of the finest recreational areas in Southeastern Kentucky. Hike, camp, fish, swim, boat or take a white-water rafting trip on the beautiful Cumberland River. Cumberland Falls State Resort Park lies amidst a breathtaking natural setting. The falls, known as the "Niagra of the South," is a tremendous wall of water falling 60-feet into a boulder-strewn gorge. During a full moon, see the only moonbow found in the Western Hemisphere.

Big South Fork National River and Recreation Area (www.bsfsry.com) encompasses rugged and scenic terrain. The 105,000 acres is filled with huge rock formations, waterfalls and fast flowing streams, deep canyons and forests. A trip to Blue Heron, a restored coal mining camp, takes visitors on a open-air train through majestic natural sights. Just minutes from I-75, the Hal Rogers Family Entertainment Center is home to the Kentucky Splash Water Park (www.kentuckysplash.com). The center includes an 18,000 square foot wave pool, a drift river, a kiddy activity pool, a triple slide complex, a go-kart track, a championship miniature golf course, an arcade, a batting cage and a driving range.

Each October Williamsburg hosts the nationally renowned Jeep Jamboree USA, which draws visitors in from Florida to California and Canada to test their four-wheel drives against mountainous terrain.

West Hwy 92
Williamsburg, KY 40769
(606) 549-6065 (866) 812-1860
www.kentuckysplash.com
www.williamsburgky.com

Kentucky Splash
Waterpark

DIRECTIONS: Take I-75 S to Exit 11 on West Hwy 92

ADMISSION: Prices vary, contact Kentucky Splash Waterpark for details

HOURS: Open Mon-Sat 11-7; Sun 12:30-6

WHITLEY COUNTY - Eastern Highlands South Region

Red River Gorge

View from Chimney Rock overlook

Natural Bridge

Journey through the Red River Gorge Geological Area and see the magnificent natural wonders of one of the most unique areas in the eastern U.S. Located in the Daniel Boone National Forest, the Red River Gorge reveals high stone cliffs and natural stone arches framing rugged forested areas, ridge-top views, waterfalls and abundant rugged beauty.

Created by the Red River, the gorge is the site for outdoor adventures including hiking, camping, fishing, canoeing, kayaking, white water rafting and wildlife watching. A popular place for rock climbing and rapelling, the gorge offers unique routes for the beginner to the experienced climber. Tour the Gladie Historic Site and see what life was like from ancient times to the turn of the century logging boom. Travel the Red River Gorge Scenic Byway (www.byways.org).

Neighboring Natural Bridge State Resort Park brings visitors to a 900-ton sandstone arch suspended 65 feet high across a mountainside, spanning 78 feet. At Natural Bridge, each season has a unique charm. Hikers are drawn to this rugged terrain, but everyone can enjoy the ridge-top views from the Natural Bridge Sky Lift. Hemlock Lodge is nestled in the mountainside, overlooking a pool complex and Hoedown Island. Log homes, chalets and cabin rentals offer a quiet retreat.

478 Washington Street
Stanton, KY 40380-2048
(606) 663-1161

Powell County
Tourism Commission

www.powellcountytourism.com

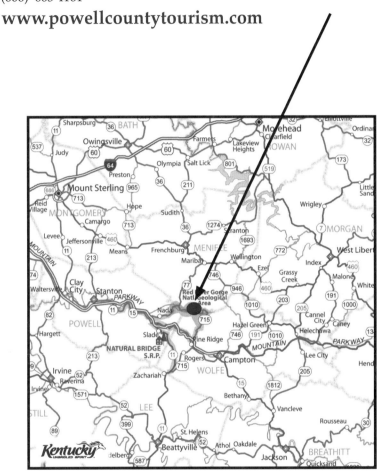

DIRECTIONS: From Lexington: take I-64 East at Exit 111 toward Ashland. Exit onto Mountain Parkway at Exit 98. Travel on Mountain Parkway to Exit 22, Stanton. Pick up byway by going north on KY 213 to junction with KY 15/11

HOURS: Open year round

Alice Lloyd College

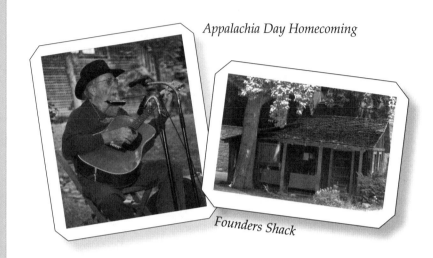

Appalachia Day Homecoming

Founders Shack

Deep within the wooded mountains of eastern Kentucky, along the banks of Caney Creek, is a college holding fast to its tradition of values and its legacy of standards. With aspirations as high as the mountains, Alice Lloyd College is a special place…with a special purpose…for special people. Founded by a courageous woman for whom the College is named, it is indeed, a light unto the mountains® – an educational community of fun and fellowship dedicated to the dignity of work, service to others and quality higher education – all encompassed by a wonderful mountain culture.

The natural beauty and rugged challenges of the Appalachian Mountains lie at the very core of the Alice Lloyd College experience. Surround yourself with the beauty and serenity of these mountains and visit Alice Lloyd College, located in the small eastern Kentucky town of Pippa Passes. Your visit to this historical educational spot will be an enjoyable learning experience for all.

Alice Lloyd College holds its annual Appalachia Day Homecoming celebration every second Saturday of October. The celebration includes exhibits and demonstrations of Appalachian arts and crafts, traditional mountain music, special alumni events, the traditional soup bean supper, children's activities, and an Appalachian authors book signing. This is a time of great fellowship and fun!

100 Purpose Road
Pippa Passes, KY 41844
(888) 280-4252
stephaniedamron@alc.edu
www.alc.edu

Alice Lloyd College

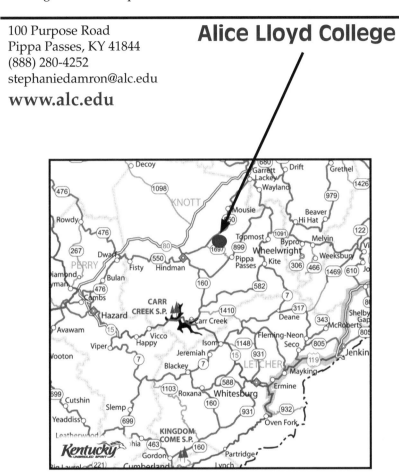

DIRECTIONS: I-75 S to Hwy 80; go right on Hwy 160, which turns into Hwy 550; left on Hwy 899 to Pippa Passes (10 miles off Hwy 80)

ADMISSION: Free self-guided walking tour anytime

HOURS: Free guided tours Mon-Fri 8-4:30 or by special appointment

A new keepsake book...

Back Home In Kentucky, Inc. is pleased to announce the release of its new book, **Kentucky's Civil War 1861-1865**. This hard cover book represents a comprehensive presentation of Kentucky's role in that tragic conflict, as interpreted by Kentucky's finest Civil War scholars and writers.

Among the book's distinguished authors are State Historian Dr. James Klotter, professors of history Dr. Lowell Harrison, Dr. James Ramage, Dr. Charles Roland, and former Poet Laureate of Kentucky Richard Taylor.

TO ORDER
KENTUCKY'S CIVIL WAR 1861-1865:

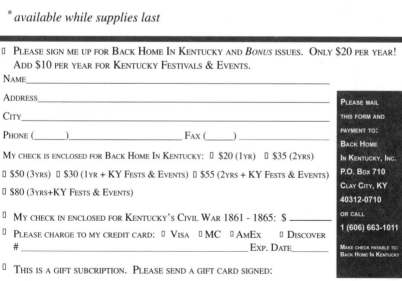

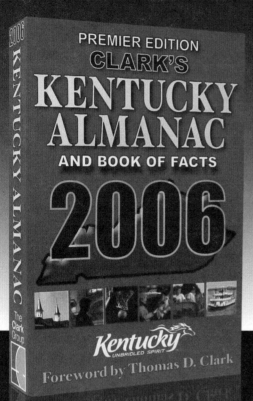

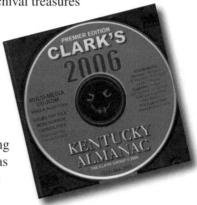